How to Tame Technol...
and Get Your Life Back

To Sarah, Rosanna and Shaunagh.

For apps, podcasts, support, training products and comment:

expertadviceonline.com

kevinduncan@expertadvice.co.uk

greatesthitsblog.com

Teach® Yourself

How to Tame Technology and Get Your Life Back

Kevin Duncan

First published in Great Britain in 2011 by Hodder Education (*as Revolution_Tame Technology_Get Your Life Back*). An Hachette UK company.

First published in US in 2011 by The McGraw-Hill Companies, Inc.

Previously published as *Revolution_Tame Technology_Get Your Life Back*

This edition published 2013 by Hodder & Stoughton. An Hachette UK company.

Copyright © Kevin Duncan

Also available in ebook

Contents

Foreword

When I was at school, we lived through a calculator arms race: bigger and bigger, more and more functions, bigger and bigger memory. Many of them are now museum pieces and the size and weight of a small laptop, but at the time they were the bleeding edge of technology.

Would the outsourcing of calculation make us stupid, teachers wondered? How could they ensure it was the student and not the machine that did the work? How could they teach us to be smart users rather than dumb slaves of the machines?

In this book, Kevin Duncan takes apart the difficulties that many of us have in dealing with the ubiquitous technology of our age, and gives us simple tips and advice on how to learn to live more comfortably with all the gadgetry that we have come to depend on.

How not to get 'muttered' and 'facetubed' into stupidity.

Brilliantly written, and a must-read.

Mark Earls, author of *Herd*

Endorsements

'Kevin Duncan really nails the problem most of us face in dealing with the technology that is shaping our world. And shows you simple and useful ways to get to grips with it. Forget Wired, buy this.'

Mark Earls, author of *Herd*

'He does for business what Nike does for sport.'

Richard Hytner, Deputy Chairman, Saatchi & Saatchi Worldwide

'Kevin Duncan has a winning way with words.'

British Airways Business Life

Introduction

In a dictionary as recently as 2003, technology is described as the application of practical sciences to industry or commerce, or the total knowledge of human skills available to any human society. These days it would include a definition based on devices that save time, enable new ways of communicating and connect communities all over the world.

Things are changing, and they are changing fast.

Technology can be a force for good – that is not in doubt. But it can also distort perspectives of what life should be all about, and that's what this book tries to address. The internet and mobile phones have become universally available in the last 15 to 20 years, which means that the world now contains millions of people who have never experienced anything else.

In training, anyone under the age of 30 is prone to ask what people did all day without these two developments. The answer, of course, is that the technology of the day was used to make arrangements and get things done, and that meant using the landline, making arrangements in advance and sticking to them. And we had more time.

This book is not about hankering after the past. It's about dealing with the present. I meet too many people who are not coping with what technology is throwing at them: too many calls, too many emails. No time to think or relax. In some cases, it has not even occurred to them that they can turn their machines off.

The equation between man and machine has to be right. If you can do more, and faster, with technology, then that should not become a reason to do even more. It should create a moment in which other activities can be pursued. As the saying goes, the moment you achieve the impossible, your boss will simply add it to your regular list of duties. No, when the job is done, it's done, and it should be a matter of human choice what we do next.

It's your life, so don't let your machines run it.

Kevin Duncan, Westminster, 2012

The road to edidction

In this chapter you will learn:

▶ *How technology and the internet have evolved over the years, and the vast amount of information being sent and received every day.*

▶ *Technology can be a wonderful thing and has transformed our lives. But it can also be a curse when it overwhelms us and begins to run our lives.*

▶ *How 'bleisure time' is a common problem for most people these days. Thanks to mobile devices we never turn off from work, being able to pick up our emails everywhere.*

▶ *That gadgets affect our self-esteem, have created a phobia of missing out and have caused us to depend on them; we are constantly up-gadgeting to keep up with the Joneses.*

▶ *How things were before this rise of technology.*

The evolution of ediction

> 'I signed on, although I never realised it, for 100,000 hours
> of work during my lifetime.... My teenage son or daughter,
> a generation later, can expect their jobs to add up, on
> average, to 50,000 hours.'
>
> Charles Handy, 1989

Glance back at any business book in the 1970s or 1980s and
you will find extremely bright people like Charles Handy
analysing the manner in which technology would revolutionize
our lives. The predictions were all the same: machines would do
wonderful things to save us the work, and as a result we would
have much more free time – this example suggests 50 per cent
more. Well here we are in the future and it hasn't quite worked
out like that. In fact, we work longer hours than ever. So how
did it come to this?

You have probably seen the cartoon sequence that shows man
rising from an ape to *Homo erectus,* and then regressing down
to a slouch until he finally comes to rest on a sofa or in front of
a computer. Starting with fire, tools and the wheel, the schematic
suggests that technology made man the most powerful species
on earth, and then weighed him back down again. It's probably
a bit much to call this the ascent and descent of man, but the
time has come to review our relationship with technology. The
industrial revolution was one thing, the internet revolution
was another, and since the invention of the World Wide Web,
mobile phones, personal computers, and every other device you
can think of, man has been confronted with a lot more than he
originally bargained for.

Don't get me wrong: technology is not a bad thing in its own
right, but individuals must be able to manage it properly if they
are to lead decent, balanced lives. 'Ediction' is my word for
being addicted to something electronic. If you are 'edicted' to
one device or several, then chances are your levels of stress will
be higher than necessary. Not being able to cope with all that
the world throws at us technologically is no disgrace, but when
it leads to unacceptable pressure and feelings of helplessness it's
time to do something about it. That's where this book comes in.

After a short run-up to establish how on earth we arrived here, we will try to find out whether you need to start to tame your technology – a complete overhaul of how the technology in your life affects you and how you approach it. The idea is relevant to young and old. Older people can learn new skills fast, and a huge number of silver surfers are already proving that. But equally we now have an entire young generation who have never experienced life *without* computers and mobile phones, and many are missing out on life skills as a result. They may wonder what people did with their time before all this technology existed. Going nostalgically dewy-eyed about playing in the street and building tree houses is not the point here – we need the ability to experience both worlds in a complementary and balanced way.

Unlock the facts

Ediction is being addicted to something electronic.

Technology can be a wonderful thing and has transformed our lives. But it can also be a curse when it overwhelms us. If your phone, computer or other devices are beginning to rule your life, then you may be edicted. It doesn't have to be like this. It's time for us humans to tame the machines and get our lives back. But first, let's see how things got to this stage.

Repetitive strain injury

'The big picture is more likely to paralyse than to inspire.'
Matthew Parris

The world arguably has too much information and many individuals can't cope. In 2007, we passed an interesting landmark. The digital universe equalled 281 billion gigabytes of data, or about 45 gigabytes for every person on earth. If that doesn't mean much to you, then you might be interested to learn that it was the first time that the overall size of digital content went beyond the total storage capacity. In other words, we were producing more online material than we could store.

Frantic increases in the size of server farms have struggled to keep up with this volume and even now only half of the digital world is stored – the rest is in transit.

Eye-watering statistics like this keep coming. An exabyte is 1.074 billion gigabytes. The internet currently handles one exabyte of data *every hour*. Inevitably, this statistic will be out of date by the time you read this. We are almost running out of the right language to describe what is happening, so let's strip it back to basics. If individuals can't cope with too much inbound information, then they need to pause and make sure the technology is working for them and not the other way round. Less is more. Understanding is everything.

The fact that we are generating so much data is both good and bad. If sought and used judiciously it can be a rich source of insight and can lead to what Clay Shirky calls a 'cognitive surplus'. For the first time ever, young people are watching less television than their elders and are instead using more of their free time for active participation in social interaction online. But many people are so swamped with information that they simply don't know what to do with it and that can lead to paralysis. In 2009, the world had generated more data than in its entire existence beforehand. That truly is a lot to take in. When people talk of information overload, they have a point. There is a limit and we may well have reached it. Take the number of people using social networks for example. If Facebook were a country it would be the third largest in the world behind China and India. It now has a staggering 1 billion active users. That's an enormous community that represents one in seven of the world's population.

The world population is itself growing by about 1 billion every 13 years, and everybody from Masai tribesmen to Mumbai students wants a phone or a computer, so we have effectively passed the point of no return when it comes to the exponential spread of technology. None of this is going to go away, so we need to develop helpful coping strategies to make sure that we are not overwhelmed by it all. If anything, it is more likely to increase in speed and intensity. So that's the big backdrop. Now let's look at the very recent past.

Technology milestones

'Experts believe the iPad will revolutionize the way we procrastinate.'

David Letterman

Humans have always had an insatiable need to invent things. Once we had the basic designs for transport, there was no stopping us: airplanes, boats, cars and space rockets. By 1990, you might have had a computer at work, and, heaven forbid, one at home. Posh executives were having phones put in their cars, which involved ripping out half of the interior. By the mid-nineties, mobile phones were becoming common. Fast forward to today and there are more mobiles in the UK than there are people.

The worldwide picture is truly extraordinary – mobile penetration has reached a vast 87 per cent of the world population. That's 6.2 billion mobile subscriptions. Even allowing for individuals having multiple phones and subscriptions, that still leaves 4.2 billion people. One manufacturer predicts that by 2017 those subscriptions will have reached 9 billion – more than the world population.

Unlock the facts

Technology is great, but not if it overwhelms us.

It seems we all love a gadget, whether for work or play. In fact, the first ten years of the current millennium are often referred to as the decade of the gadget, and the top ten most popular, in chronological order, were:

USB stick (2000)
IBM launched the DiskOnKey, thereby condemning the floppy disk to the history books, and the bin. It soon became the quickest way to transfer files between computers.

Apple iPod (2001)
This machine has totally changed the way in which we consume music. Originally only capable of holding 1,000 songs, it has now become a multi-media receptacle.

Sky+ (2001)
No need for tapes or careful planning and programming of recorders. This easy-to-use box with a large hard drive allowed viewers to record hundreds of hours of programmes at the touch of a button.

BlackBerry (2002)
Loathed and revered in equal measure, this mobile email device meant life would never be the same for many. Fans love the 'always on' functionality – families and partners less so.

TomTom Go (2004)
Goodbye maps, hello satellite navigation. Ideal for those with no sense of direction, until they take it too literally and end up driving into a lake.

Slingbox (2005)
A television streaming device that allows you to shift (sling) shows from your TV or video recorder to a computer anywhere in the world.

Nintendo Wii (2006)
This family-orientated games console arguably introduced a whole new generation to video games. To date, 56 million sold and rising.

Flip (2007)
A pocket-sized camcorder that can capture about an hour of footage. The built-in USB stick flips out, allowing editing and uploading to the web. Much loved by YouTube users, now anyone can be an on-the-spot journalist.

Asus Eee PC (2007)
Not the world's most well-known brand name, but this ultra-light laptop kick-started the netbook genre – a new category of basic computers for sending emails and using the internet on the go, usually for less than £200.

iPhone (2007)
The mobile phone was now totally redefined and responsible for more than a billion apps being downloaded since the launch of the App Store in 2009.

This extraordinary list almost needs no further comment. Suffice to say that these gadgets, and scores of others, have completely changed the way in which humans operate, and if you were born in the last ten or twenty years, all this is the norm. The gadgets run parallel with ingenious online social networks such as Twitter, which launched in July 2006, and LinkedIn, with its slow burn build from 2003 to a community of 175 million.

Many trainees have never heard of a fax, photocopiers are almost obsolete and many people have no idea that CC stands for a carbon copy. A recent 22-year-old recruit to Apple had never used email because his life was run purely by mobile phone and social media. Indeed, the role of machines is so profound that they have even blurred the distinction between what is leisure and what is business.

The rise of bleisure time

'It's not the prettiest word, but you'd better get used to it because this blurring between our working lives and downtime, or business and leisure, is here to stay.'

Tony Turnbull

The rise of bleisure can be viewed in two ways. If we choose to let it be, our world is 'always on'. That's good if you want to play music and watch films, and bad if you can never mentally leave the office. If you use your iPhone to play a game or download some music, in all likelihood you will also see a new stream of office emails. With iron discipline you could isolate the one from the other, but in fact few people can resist the temptation to have a look – even though they know that what they discover may not necessarily make them happy. The tools of work and play have effectively become one and the traditional nine-to-five has effectively ceased to exist. People take business calls in the evening and visit eBay from their desks, if the company system lets them.

Separating life and work has become a lost skill. Maybe this should not come as a surprise though; we are all born to play and create, according to Pat Kane, author of *The Play Ethic*. He suggests that politicians arguing consistently for a work ethic are missing the point. We are essentially designed to play. We all think we know what play is (what we do as children, outside work and for no other reason than pleasure), but understanding the real meaning of it would revolutionize and liberate our daily lives. Play offers learning, progress, imagination, a sense of self, identity and contest. It is also the fermenting ground for exploring alternatives – the very essence of creativity.

Unlock the facts

The tools of work and play have effectively become one.

Huge numbers of companies have caught on to this idea and now make their money out of play elements. This is good news if a new generation of workers can get paid for doing something they enjoy, and the more work is like play, the more likely this is to be the case. Corporations and governments have embraced this notion in the idea of so-called 'gamification' – a process in which serious or commercial messages are conveyed through the medium of a game. In other words, people are more likely to take something in if it is encapsulated in the medium of a game. It is not yet clear whether this is purely down to our play characteristics or the pervasive power of the technology that presents them.

Technology needs careful handling where the work ethic slams into the play ethic. Millions of working hours are lost in companies around the world as employees muck about on websites, chat rooms, social media and more. Companies try to stop it, but only partially succeed. The idea of work/life balance has become confusing. The difference between work and play in a technological world has become blurred. You would have thought that those who spend all day at work on a computer would want to do something else in their spare time, but often they just do more of it when they get home. Using technology can be addictive, and doing so is a form of consumption in its own right.

Enough: have we over-consumed?

'Am I being up-gadgeted? Masses of planetary resources get piled into adding features to make our lives easier. But do they really add anything? If they don't, then we are just spending money on landfill.'

John Naish

John Naish, author of *Enough,* points out that our basic survival strategy makes us chase more of everything: status, food, information and possessions. Now, thanks to a mixture of technology and money, we have suddenly got more of everything than we can ever use. As a result, we urgently need to develop a sense of 'enough', and an ability to enjoy what we have, rather than fixating on 'more'. This frequently applies to the purchase of clothes, for example; in truth we only need a certain amount but often we just keep on filling the wardrobe.

Scientists have shown that purchasing items gives us a dopamine rush but it wears off almost immediately. Thousands of women in particular routinely return everything on a Monday that they bought on Saturday. Retailers call them shoe-limics. WILFing is a pointless form of shopping: *What Was I Looking For?* In this case the activity, not the purchase, has become the point. Technology addicts can suffer from the same phenomenon, buying more and more gadgets whether they are 'needed' or not. 'All the gear but no idea' is how one sports equipment shop owner describes his fair-weather customers, and the phrase could equally apply to anyone with too many technological devices. These people are most likely edicted.

When it comes to data and information, many of us are suffering from 'infobesity'. Too much information causes stress and confusion and makes people do irrational things. For example, our 24-hour news media suffers from an 'Elvis still dead' syndrome that distorts our view of the world to the point that many of us have effectively forgotten what true news is. We keep on consuming it until we become bloated with too much information.

Developing a sense of enough is also necessary at work. As we saw at the beginning of the book, we were expected to be working less by now, thanks to the power of technology, but actually we are working more. This is partly because of the blurriness of bleisure time, but also because some of us have developed a warped attitude to work. 'Presenteeism' is a phenomenon whereby people spend hours at their desks not achieving anything because they are too tired, stressed, under-stimulated, distracted or depressed to be productive. Workaholics Anonymous is a movement based on Alcoholics Anonymous principles. Ironically, when they tried the scheme in New York, only two people turned up because the rest were too busy. In another extreme paradox, earning more simply increases discontentment. Many people believe (or convince themselves) that their overwork habits are driven by irresistible external forces. They then frown on normal timekeepers and make their lives a misery.

Has all this consumption made people any happier? No it hasn't. But amazingly people always think things will be better in the future. Present quality of life is deemed to be 6.9 out of 10 (and guessed at 8.2 in five years' time). But when the time comes, it will still be 6.9. In many instances, this over-consumption is a case of too much too soon, and in some cases, too much full stop. Customer demands are being met fast, and are followed immediately by the creation of, and satiating of, even more technological demands. Some gadgets appear to fill needs that people previously never even knew they had.

Remember this

Are you constantly up-gadgeting? Sixty per cent of adults use less than half of the functions on their devices.

Are you constantly up-gadgeting? Sixty per cent of adults use less than half of the functions on their devices. If any of this rings a bell with you and your approach to technology, then you may be edicted. Many people in this state of affairs feel trapped in an inexorable vortex in which they are being asked to do more and more and being given technology that in theory enables them to fulfil those demands. In practice, however, they can't cope. As the saying goes, the moment you achieve the impossible for your boss, they simply add it to your regular list of duties. The sheer volume of inbound material has in many cases reached a point where it cannot be dealt with. In fast-moving businesses, it is not uncommon for executives to receive 100 emails an hour. Even sitting and hitting delete as fast as they come in would not handle the volume.

Case study: Technology Time Machine 1980

It's 1980. The mobile phone doesn't exist, unless you count those field telephones that they used to use in the war. A few such devices exist and are used on rural film shoots. The batteries weigh as much as a bag of bricks and only last for half an hour or so. Email hasn't been invented yet. The car phone won't be along for another eight years or so. If you want to talk to someone it's a landline or a phone box.

Steve works in an advertising agency. It's classified as a fairly pacey job. So what does Steve do all day? Here's a snapshot of his working day.

The alarm clock wakes him up – it's one of those modern ones with a digital display, but it's not an LED (light-emitting diode) because they have only just been invented and are still too expensive for commercial use. It's easy walking from the underground to the office because everyone is looking where they are going – no one is looking down at their mobile devices because no one has one. He can hear everything too because no one is wearing headphones, although Steve is looking forward to playing his cassettes on a Sony Walkman when they come out next year.

Arriving at the office, there are a couple of hand-written messages from the switchboard lady, so he calls his clients on the landline. They discuss business and agree when they will meet next. This afternoon's meeting has been delayed by two hours, which will mean he'll be home later than usual. He calls his wife to let her know but she isn't in and he can't leave a message because they don't have an answering machine – there are one or two on the market but they are too expensive for the average household budget. He'll have to try again later.

On the way to the client meeting the car breaks down. There's no way to call the breakdown services so they flag down another motorist and grab a lift to the nearest phone box. Steve only has a few 10p pieces so he has to be brief and describe their location accurately. He doesn't have enough coins left to call the client and explain they will be late. Once the car is fixed, they are safely on their way and the meeting carries on with the client being sympathetic. Steve persuades one of the secretaries to let him use her landline to call his wife and this time he gets through.

A little later Steve's wife would love to call and suggest he pick up some dessert to round off the evening meal, but there's no way of contacting him, and anyway the shops shut at 6 p.m. so things will just have to stay as they are. After dinner, they sit down to watch television and there is a choice of three channels (Channel 4 doesn't launch until 2 November 1982). It's a pretty straightforward life with no communication devices enabling last-minute changes.

Steve gets a decent night's sleep, knowing that the only thing that can disturb him is an emergency on the landline.

Affluenza and ediction

'Ten years ago, we'd happily queue in a bank to get £50. Now, if you're standing at a cash machine and one person is pressing the receipt button, you actually want to kill them.'

Simon Cowell

It is now beyond doubt that we buy more technology than we need. We want a lot and we want it fast. *Affluenza* is defined by Oliver James as a contagious middle-class virus causing depression, addiction and ennui. This is an epidemic sweeping the world and in order to counteract it and ensure our mental health we should pursue our needs rather than our wants – the majority of which are unsustainable.

Most middle class people have too much of everything, he says, but it hasn't made them any happier. People need to reject much of the status quo in order to be a satisfied, unstressed individual. We have become more miserable and distressed since the 1970s, thanks to successive governments pushing the cause of personal capitalism. While there has been a massive increase in the wealth of the wealthy, there has been no rise in average wages. We need to recapture a sense of self-worth and personal well-being if we are to overcome these negative feelings. Erich Fromm's theory of American consumerism states that the choice in the 1950s was 'to have or to be', and that people have become marketing characters 'based on experiencing oneself as a commodity'. Arguably, nothing much has changed.

Technology can help with much of this if used wisely. Equally, it is worth remembering that humans only really have four basic needs: to feel safe and secure, to feel competent, to feel connected to others, and to feel autonomously and authentically engaged in work and play. Earning more creates a desire for more technology and self-doubt correlates with materialism. Interestingly, everyone feels that 'enough' income is always ten per cent more than they have. The range of goods regarded as 'essential' in a household has also increased dramatically, as has the speed with which they can be obtained – in an on-demand world, everybody wants everything now.

Technology feeds this need and everybody is getting impatient. Time is being squeezed in a concertina. The faster it comes, the faster you want it next time. This speed demand works in two directions. Consumers order something online and expect it to turn up tomorrow. Equally, those working in companies are expected to respond immediately. Email is not technically a fast-response medium (you don't know if the other person is there right now), and yet many executives are chastised if an email is not met with a response within five minutes, thereby reducing their jobs to little more than that of a technological rapid response unit akin to a call centre, regardless of their specific expertise. And yet, as Gandhi pointed out, 'There is more to life than increasing its speed.'

Phobology and self-esteem

> 'Technology is a queer thing: it brings you great gifts with one hand, and stabs you in the back with the other.'
>
> C. P. Snow

Phobology is the study of phobias, and we have a lot of them. The top five phobias in the UK, in reverse order, are: driving (1 per cent), erythrophobia – that's blushing (1.2 per cent), emetophobia – vomit (2.6 per cent), agoraphobia (9.9 per cent), and at number one is social phobia at 17.2 per cent. Technology has played a role in this, both good and bad. On the plus side, it has opened up networks for shy people, allowed internet dating, helped those with learning difficulties, provided instant messaging capability for those in therapy who don't want to talk on the phone, and much more. On the minus side, it can allow people to hide behind it, reduce face-to-face interaction and build barriers in relationships. As Erik Qualman claims in his book *Socialnomics,* 'the next generation can't speak.' If you would rather email your wife than talk to her, then things may be going wrong, but you won't be alone. Twenty-five per cent of UK adults now check their electronic device in the morning in bed before saying good morning to their partner.

Unlock the facts

When it comes to data and information, we are suffering from infobesity.

The launch of endless new products can lead to paranoia and reduced self-esteem. More and more choice might mean 50 brands of cooking oil, 200 brands of beer, 500 TV channels and tens of thousands of websites. This all sounds rather wonderful at first glance, but the American sociologist Barry Schwartz has studied product proliferation and believes that, after a certain point, too much choice overloads our brains. 'Increased choice may actually contribute to the recent epidemic of clinical depression affecting much of the western world,' he says in *The Paradox of Choice.* He was rather dismayed to find 16 varieties of instant mashed potatoes in his local supermarket. Science writer James Gleick reached the same conclusion, lamenting that the more telephone lines you have, the more you need. The complications beget choice; the choice inspires technology; the technologies create complication. It's a never-ending cycle.

Keeping up with the Joneses has always been a messy and soul-destroying business, and proliferation of choice makes it worse. Consider the role of technology in fuelling this phenomenon. A household in the 1950s might aspire to a radio, a fridge and possibly a food mixer. The average kitchen now has every conceivable feature, and may even include a fridge with an integrated digital shopping list. One television set per house is now inconceivable and there may well be one in your car or in your hand. The screen in your living room is probably now an all-in entertainment system. Many people have several phones and more than one version of what is effectively the same device. But this proliferation is not uniform. One in five Americans have never sent an email.

Convergence brings convenience and pleasure on the one hand, and heartbreak and stress on the other. How convenient it is to have your phone, email, contacts, messages, important data, diary and hundreds of other vital items on your hand-held device – until you lose it. 'I couldn't live without my phone' is the mantra of the modern generation. Few have landlines, alarm clocks, watches, diaries or any other old-fashioned paraphernalia. Their whole life is concentrated on one omnipotent device – until it gets stolen, falls down the toilet or just stops working. This is not necessarily a tale of woe. It just needs putting in perspective. Self-esteem and inner confidence should come before total dependence on any piece of technology. No one should depend on any single thing that much, be it human or machine. Which begs the question: do you?

Are you in love with a machine?

'The odds are good but the goods are odd.'

Online dating customer

There's nothing wrong with online dating and it has certainly generated high levels of satisfaction for many looking for a partner. As with many things in life, it works well if handled sensitively, notwithstanding the witty observation that the odds are good but the goods are odd. On reflection, that could just as easily be the case when dating anyone, regardless of where you met. Falling in love when you have met someone is great, but is it okay to be in love with a machine? Do you know anyone who is? Are you yourself? These questions aren't as daft as they may sound. Humans, and particularly men, have always loved machines. There are devoted enthusiasts for trains, planes, cars, boats, motorbikes and hundreds of others. These days technological advances have made many of these machines more appealing to both sexes, to young and old, and have made them pervade every walk of life. Many relationships have been lost to those with obsessive hobbies that drive their partners mad and make them feel excluded, and modern devices have exacerbated the problem.

Computer games, mobile phones, personal organizers, laptops, email or even just the ability to work at home have ripped apart many a partnership. So when someone stares admiringly at their iPad, is it love? It might well be, and if it is, it could be a dangerous moment for the admirer. And there are probably a lot of them. To put this in perspective, it took Apple over six years to sell a million of its Apple II computers after launching in 1977. The iMac achieved that milestone in just over a year in 1998, as did the iPod in 2001. The iPhone sold a million in 74 days in 2007. The iPad did it in 28 days, and has now sold over 80 million units so far, creating a new tablet category in the process. James Lileks drily noted that 'the iPad is the Barack Obama of technology. It's whatever you want it to be, until you actually get it.'

There is nothing wrong with these sales figures, nor the machines. In fact, they are brilliantly clever. I own plenty of them myself. The critical question is what they mean to the individual. If they mean connection, freedom of expression, ability to interact with others as never before, and a host of other benefits, then clearly that's a good thing. All that benefit, however, relies on the user keeping a balanced approach to how much time they spend interacting with the technology, whether that represents a sensible ratio in relation to pursuing other activities and whether those around them – friends, partners and family – find that level of interaction healthy and acceptable.

All of which leaves the modern human with much to ponder. Technology has always been creeping up on us, but now it has come upon us like a tidal wave. The new so-called 'digital natives' embrace it with open arms and know no other way of living. Those who are a little older may find much of it daunting. There is no system with which to judge what a sensible level of involvement with one's technology might be, so it falls to the individual themselves to take a sensible view. You can start by asking yourself whether you are edicted. If you are not sure, then the symptoms suggested in the next chapter, and the test that goes with it, might help you decide.

Focus points

✷ The evolution of ediction has taken a while to creep up on us. Instead of accepting things as they are, it's worth taking the time to consider whether how you currently interact with technology is acceptable. It may be time to reconsider.

✷ The rise of bleisure time is confusing and serves to complicate matters. Most mobile devices mix business and pleasure in ways that often add stress, so it pays to disentangle the two if you can.

✷ Have you over-consumed? Most people have far more than they need. It's a good discipline to pause and reflect. A clear-out of unused or unwanted possessions – many of them technological – can be therapeutic. This enables a clean start, on your terms.

✷ Phobology and self-esteem are interrelated thoughts. Among the many phobias that people have is a fear of missing out or not being in demand. Technology helps feed this phobia with its incessant demand for updates and provision of news. But self-esteem can be derived from sources other than technology. Determining the purpose of your various devices is a good place to start.

✷ Are you in love with a machine? It's a rather strange question but many relationships have suffered because someone is paying an undue amount of attention to a device rather than their partner. Technology can be wonderful, but it's not the only thing in the world. Start by recalibrating your attitude to technology alongside the other things that matter in life.

Next step

Chapter 2 moves on to look at whether you need to tame your technology and includes a test to see how badly you are addicted to it.

Do you need to tame your technology?

In this chapter you will learn:

- ▶ *If you are controlling your technology or if your technology is controlling you.*
- ▶ *How technology takes over your life: phone calls, emails, text messages – they all demand an instant response.*
- ▶ *How face-to-face conversations are suffering, either by terse and anonymous immediacy of a computer-driven exchange, or when chatting in person, suffering from 'continuous partial attention' that is caused by always having one eye on your mobile.*
- ▶ *That due to the demand for instant response, technological interventions can have a huge bearing on what you can achieve.*
- ▶ *That it's easy to hide behind technology, and this isn't always a good thing.*

So we know that technology can cause a lot of trouble if it remains untamed. If a person is addicted to technology then they are edicted. Is this you? Are you controlling your technology, or is it the other way round? You can take the test at the end of this chapter to find out how bad things are and decide whether you need to start a revolution in your life. But first let's look at some of the different ways in which your technology can start to take over your life. Interruptions can come at any time. Phone calls always could, but at least you had to be within earshot of a landline phone. These days your mobile could ring any time day or night, assuming you have left it on. Texts and instant messages ping incessantly. Texts can arrive from people and companies you have never even heard of. Emails arrive at work in an endless stream. And they tumble into your personal inbox, often as unwanted spam. Now let's examine the main culprits.

'I can't talk now; I'm on the phone...'

Do you ever interrupt a conversation with your partner or children to take a call?

You walk into the reception area of a hotel or business, and it often happens. You are talking to the receptionist, the phone rings and they break off your conversation mid-sentence to answer it. It's rude, and it demonstrates the power of interruption by technology. Why would anyone believe that the inbound intervention would be a better option than the real conversation they are currently engaged in?

In the modern world, we can all be guilty. We used to have two-way conversations when one person spoke to another and their concentration was total. Now we often have three-way conversations in which one party is probably fiddling with a device. In some cases both might be, making it a four-way conversation, or arguably not a conversation at all. As one frustrated partner put it to her other half: 'If you talk to me, I expect eye contact. Meanwhile you are typing some meaningless observation into the ether.' It has been said that mobiles and the internet have opened up the world on the one hand, only to shrink our horizon to two inches on the other – the size of the screen on our devices.

Research shows that many people now regularly keep their devices by their beds at night. Relationship counsellors talk of marriages breaking up through lack of consideration. Many partners feel they are being excluded if their partner is spending a lot of time using phones for socializing, playing games or working. Psychologists have observed that there is something quite compelling about contemporary gadgetry. Modern gadgets activate a part of the brain that wants to be absolutely absorbed. This creates a strange altered state in which the user is with their partner physically but not available to them mentally.

New symptoms have been created. *Obsessive mobile disorder* (OMD) has been joined by *continuous partial attention* (CPA), in which victims come to believe that life via mobile might in fact be more interesting than the life right in front of them. Stressful and inefficient, CPA is a never-ending effort not to miss anything, which can never be satisfactorily achieved. There's nothing wrong with staying in the picture but the sheer volume of information in the modern world makes this effectively impossible. Those who choose to make technology their centre of gravity can find it impossible to keep up.

Unlock the facts

Obsessive mobile disorder and continuous partial attention happen when people think life on their device will be more interesting than what is in front of them.

Attempting to pay attention to everything at once can have significant social implications, many of them anti-social. Jennifer Aniston once famously dumped her boyfriend John Mayer for paying more attention to his mobile than to her. The actor Richard Griffiths, finding himself interrupted several times when performing on stage in London, turned to the audience and demanded: 'Could the person whose mobile phone it is please leave? The 750 people here would be fully justified in suing you for ruining their afternoon.'

These examples affect other people, but the worst consequence may well be for oneself. When a fashion stylist admits in a newspaper that 'I couldn't live without my mobile phone,' most right-minded people know it's time to pause and think harder about the way we handle technology.

Do you have a balanced relationship with your phone?

Yr msgs r kllg me: the tyranny of text and Twitter

Have you ever regretted sending a text or email?

Texting has somewhat unusual technical origins. It was included as a throwaway feature on early mobile phones and none of the manufacturers thought many people would be bothered to manoeuvre their thumbs in all sorts of contorted patterns just to string a sentence together when it would be quicker to hit speed dial and talk. But the idea caught on in an unprecedented way. Americans send over 4 billion text messages a day and Brits 1 billion. The volumes are phenomenal, and the technology keeps developing. Original SMS (Short Message Service) communications were restricted to simple ones such as 'Happy Christmas'. Now the recipient might receive a video clip or picture of a naked friend, or possibly a footballer.

The ubiquity of mobile devices and the rapidity of texting have generated a total change in social behaviour. In days gone by, a date meant specifying when and where in order to make the tryst work. *The Dog and Duck at eight on Tuesday* may well have been teed up several days in advance on a landline, and changing the arrangement was often out of the question on the grounds that the other person could not be contacted. Studies show that, having arranged such a rendezvous, the maximum amount of time anyone was prepared to wait was 12 minutes. This precision and reliability has been replaced with the infuriatingly vague *I'll text you when I'm in the area,* leaving many a frustrated partner or mate twiddling their thumbs for hours, possibly sitting in the wrong venue.

Changing social behaviour is complicated. One twenty-something girl who was notoriously always 30 minutes late decided to mend her ways and start turning up on time, all to no avail because all her mates assumed she would always be late and so added half an hour to any proposed meeting time.

Unlock the facts

Modern gadgets activate a part of the brain that wants to be absolutely absorbed.

Many a relationship has ended in a vitriolic burst on SMS. It's fast and furious, and can be delivered at pretty much the same speed as a vicious insult to the face. And of course, phones do not come with a 'disengage when drunk' button. This might please young stags on a Saturday night when they 'text the ex' and get a positive response, but may be less appealing if insulting the boss and hugely regretting it later. Not that companies have a great track record in this area either – there have been many scandals involving text voting on TV programmes, and one company famously fired a large proportion of its staff using SMS.

Tweeting is a close cousin of texting and encourages brevity with a maximum of 140 characters per tweet. Tweets are only invasive if the recipient remains constantly tuned in to Twitter or insists on having alerts set up. Where the similarity becomes interesting is in the sending of a short message that is then almost instantly regretted. The text hits the recipient's inbox and that's the end of it because it cannot be unsent. Tweets can be deleted but, as in the recent case of a footballer's outburst, can also be retweeted 19,000 times before being removed. Any remedial action is inevitably too late and the damage is done.

Apart from social difficulties, obsessive texting can have more sinister implications. Many teenagers die every year when crossing the road looking at the message they are writing or receiving rather than the traffic and a number of government campaigns have highlighted these dangers. Worst of all, a woman was jailed in the UK in 2009 for hitting and killing a pedestrian while driving at 70 mph. She had been sending a text at the time.

Do you text or tweet too much?

Thousands of emails but no conversations?

Do you check emails for several hours a day?

They may be the brightest and the best, but they are not necessarily the nicest. That was the conclusion of a research study into the behaviour of college students in the USA. Apparently, their concern for other people's feelings is in sharp decline, leading to a *Generation Me* of self-centred, narcissistic and competitive individuals. The study concluded that the shift has been particularly noticeable in the last decade or so, probably as a consequence of growing up with violent video games, online friend networks and an obsession with TV celebrities.

The tyranny of email keeps us in touch, but also has the ability to drive us all apart. When 1.9 billion people send 294 billion emails every day, there is no doubt that we are edicted to chatting, but are we really saying anything? John Freeman argues that email encourages us to eschew face-to-face conversations with friends or colleagues in favour of the terse and anonymous immediacy of a computer-driven exchange. Psychologists note that users of modern technology are often driven by the same gambler's instinct that motivates someone to play a slot machine. You never know when something is going to land in your inbox so there is a tingle of excitement every time you check.

The modern office is a case in point. Having trained over 3,000 people in the last five years in how to cope with this onslaught, some interesting patterns emerge: 10,000 emails in the inbox was a 2008 record. This has just been surpassed at 60,000. One hundred emails per day was extreme five years ago. Now 100 an hour is not uncommon. Emailing team members sitting at the next desk is rife. Using CC (carbon copy!) to all and sundry as a backside-covering tactic is commonplace. In one company we introduced a NICE day (No Internal Calls or Emails) with a £1 penalty payable to charity for any transgressors. One individual couldn't help himself and ended up handing over £100.

Using pen and paper provides one alternative to an email culture. A US study has shown that members of Congress pay very little attention to emails, classifying them on the same level as mass mailings and petitions. Personal letters and visits are regarded as much more powerful. And how about talking to people in person? We are becoming what psychologists call 'desocialized', losing the ability to take time away from our devices and communicate properly face-to-face.

As with any form of technology, email suffers tremendously from being used as the wrong medium. Placing the right message in the right medium is crucial to ensure that it is appropriate and effective. On many occasions, people send what may well be the right message but in the wrong medium. Any message that involves significant emotion or severe news is unlikely to suit email. Think *I love you, You're fired,* or *I hate this.*

Do you send or receive too many emails?

Case study: The Edicted Couple

Roger and Catherine were the ideal couple. He worked in marketing and she was a big wheel in an investment company. They had no kids and so fitted the DINKY description perfectly (Dual Income No Kids Yet). That all adds up to a lot of disposable cash and no onerous family responsibilities. So the conditions were set perfectly for a balanced lifestyle with an appropriate blend of work and leisure time.

But strangely they didn't seem to have as much time as they wanted to spend together. Catherine usually got up at 5.30 a.m. and checked her BlackBerry for messages from clients and colleagues. She'd be in by 7 a.m. to catch the morning financial markets opening and then it was solid client work all day – occasionally interspersed with a working lunch.

Roger could get up a bit later and sometimes did. But in truth, by the time she was up, he might as well get up himself. He either checked his emails at home before driving to work or on his mobile at the gym while on the running machine. This gave him a head start on the issues of the day before he got into the office. Then it was usually back-to-back meetings all day. In the gaps he could grab a coffee or a sandwich and see what inbound email was piling up. He would answer as much of it on the hoof as he could, but in truth there was little time to think and before he knew it, it was home time.

It would have been nice if the shutters came down on work when they left the office, but they didn't. Both found that bringing work home was the norm. There was always something else to deal with. It was either a backlog of emails that needed answering before the next day's relentless programme of events or some proper thinking time needed for a presentation that would never get written at the office.

With a typical returning home time of around 7.30 p.m., they usually allowed an hour or so for some dinner, assuming they overlapped with each other, which only happened a night or two a week. Then it was back to the emails and laptop tasks – sometimes parked in front of a mindless TV programme. They might well be sitting on the sofa together but it didn't mean they were talking to each other. The volume of work spilling into leisure time left precious little room for conversation or a decent catch up – a luxury that was usually delayed until the weekend or some calmer time such as a weekend break.

Roger and Catherine were not untypical. They probably wouldn't describe themselves as edicted, and yet their technology pretty much dominates their domestic agenda. In a simpler time, the majority of their work tasks would have had to be completed at the office, but in a modern era they are expected to be 'always on'. This is partly because their employers deliberately provide all their electronic devices for free – including all the airtime and service charges. In return they expect near-permanent availability, particularly in Roger's case, who has a boss who never seems to sleep and often sends emails in the small hours.

Nowadays, these circumstances are regarded as 'normal'. This kind of learned helplessness may feel alright to Roger and Catherine but it is unlikely to be sustainable in the long run. So it is their choice if they wish to tame their technology.

Distraction or action?

Do you find yourself distracted by social media sites when you should be doing something else?

In a study in 2007, Microsoft workers took an average of 15 minutes to return to what they were doing after they were interrupted by an incoming email or instant message. Once interrupted, they strayed off to reply to other messages or browse news, sports or entertainment websites. There is a huge difference between a planned and intentional action and one taken as a result of a distraction. Many of us are now suffering from an attention deficit syndrome – one in which we are so occupied dealing with the inbound that we are almost constantly off track. At any given moment, it is worth the individual knowing what they are concentrating on and whether that is what they originally had in mind.

According to James Harkin, slaves to *Cyburbia* live in a virtual village frittering away their lives sending messages across the ether, playing chess with people they will never meet or dreaming up witty status updates on their profiles on Facebook. In Britain alone over 250 million hours a month are spent on social networking sites. The number believed to be addicted to the internet in China is 10 million, and in 2010, 14 internet addicts fled a boot camp designed to wean them off it by tying up a guard and breaking out. That's real ediction for you.

Unlock the facts

It takes an average of 15 minutes to return to what you were doing before being interrupted.

The number of drivers using mobiles and hand-held devices continues to rise, despite the obvious dangers – they are supposed to be engaged in a specific action (driving) and are actively choosing a distraction. If you cannot resist answering your device as soon as it rings, you are likely to be suffering from *distraction overload*. And what's more, several studies show that interruptions impair creativity and memory. Individuals could do worse than pause to consider which is more important: what they originally intended to do or the thing they were subsequently distracted by.

Do you find yourself easily distracted by technology?

Everything louder than everything else

Have you ever failed to notice what someone was doing or saying because you were concentrating on your phone or computer?

Distraction is one thing, and may be momentary. *Information Anxiety*, as identified by Richard Saul Wurman in the book of the same name, could be a more permanent state of affairs. As he famously showed, a weekday edition of the *New York Times* contains more information than the average person was likely to come across in a lifetime in 17th-century England.

Electricity reached a quarter of Americans 46 years after its introduction. Telephones took 35 years and television 26. It took broadband just six years.

It took two centuries to fill the shelves of the Library of Congress with more than 57 million manuscripts, 29 million books and 12 million photographs. Now the world generates the same amount of digital information 100 times a day. The scale and speed of these developments is mind-boggling and the individual is entitled to ask whether they can cope with it if they feel that everything is sounding louder than everything else.

Technology is now so pervasive that Indians are more likely to have access to a mobile phone than a lavatory (563 million vs. 366 million). Meanwhile the Germans, who have something of a knack for finding a long word to describe a particular phenomenon, often suffer from *Freizeitstresse* – free time that makes you more stressed than work. In a switched-on world, they try to take time off but become more and more anxious when they are on holiday because they perpetually feel they are out of the loop. As the desire to be 'always on' becomes pervasive, many busy executives have concluded that they would rather take their devices on holiday and check them at least once a day than not take them and return to a crisis or a mountain of work that negates the holiday. Their partners do not always agree that this is beneficial.

Do you sometimes feel overwhelmed by your technology?

It's all the (techno) rage

Have you ever become deeply angry and frustrated by technology?

Road rage is a well-documented phenomenon and no one disputes that it exists because most people have seen it in action. Techno rage is a bit more obscure – often it happens in the privacy of someone's home, when they feel that they want to destroy their computer. Crashes and lost documents are major causes. Mobile devices can contribute to stress simply because they are the conduit of news, and as we all know, not all news is good news. Certain mobile ringtones have been found to symbolize and trigger stress, either because the listener has come to associate the noise with trouble or because the ubiquity of the noise in public places represents a reminder of intrusion on privacy. One mobile phone manufacturer found both to be true of its most popular ringtone.

In a modern world, many think that they can handle it all at once, when in fact they probably can't. There must be physical and mental limits with regard to how much technological input one person can take and we may have reached these limits. However, some scientists believe that our reliance on the web for information and communication might even be changing the way we think – literally. Browsing the web for extended periods is believed to affect our neural pathways with implications for the way we respond to information and form memories. By skimming the surface of knowledge we cover more but absorb less, says one school of thought. If that is true, then exercising the mind is better achieved by concentrating on one thing at a time. But science remains divided on this.

The myth of multitasking has become a hot debate. Studies show that the most persistent multitaskers perform badly in a variety of tasks. They don't focus as well, they are more easily distractible and they are weaker at shifting from one thing to another. They often have a lot of tasks started but not necessarily completed. In fact, they are worse at it than people who do *not* usually multitask. And yet having a lot on the go at once has become something of a badge of honour in its own right with some employers specifically demanding it.

Pretty much everyone has experienced angry helplessness when technology breaks down. If we have not experienced it directly (although we probably have), we all know someone who has become distraught after leaving their mobile in a cab, failing to get a signal, losing a crucial document on a laptop or running out of battery power somewhere inconvenient. It's modern life. We need a new approach to improve our ability to cope. Mounting frustration inevitably leads to poor decisions, stress and often confrontation or declining health.

Do you get frustrated by technology?

Hiding behind technology

Have you ever used technology to avoid talking face-to-face?

As we saw in the last chapter, technology has played a part in what many believe to be a decline in social skills. Arguments for technology helping in this area are removal of social stigma, heightened awareness of what is happening beyond one's front door, the development of certain creative skills and even the ability to find a suitable partner via internet dating. Almost every perceived benefit, however, has a negative counterpoint that can be cited. Detractors point to reduced face-to-face interaction, anonymity that can lead to stalking, cybercrime, addictive gambling, online scams, online bullying and a generation of users who struggle to interact successfully with the outside world.

Some people actively hide behind technology. The worse the news, the more likely it is to come via a computer or device.

Looking someone dead in the eye and delivering bad news has never been easy. Now, if it's too painful to deliver in person, people can send a text, email, instant message or just leave a message. *You're dumped* seems to be a case in point. More annoyingly for the recipient, multiple channels often lead to multiple messages – all about the same thing: *I just rang to check if you'd got my text about the email I sent you?* Colleagues who want to cover their backs are major culprits here – everything seems to be delivered in triplicate to prove that it's your problem, not theirs. In a business context, this gets the issue out of your inbox and onto someone else's desk.

Unlock the facts

Many people actively hide behind technology.

Technology can also provide scale to blur social distinctions. Three hundred 'friends' on Facebook may or may not mean what it says. Most studies show that the maximum number of viable 'friends' anyone can have is 150, with a tight circle of around five friends, expanding out to a sympathy group of fifteen or so, to the remainder who are people we loosely know. Can the power of social media transcend the normal maths of how many relationships one person can realistically sustain? Some observers believe that such technology merely provides a new platform for bragging rights with regard to social popularity and business importance.

Studies have shown that the primary purpose of the hand-held device is to increase the self-esteem of the owner. For under-confident people this may be no bad thing, but for those who are not short of bravado, or who lack subtlety, it could be unpleasant for all concerned. As Tom Peters has observed: 'If you are constantly on your BlackBerry, it is mostly because of an arrogant, consuming sense of self-importance totally divorced from reality. The world will not come to an end if you are out of touch for 20 minutes. Or an hour. Or a day.'

Do you ever hide behind technology?

Can't get no satisfaction
(even in topless meetings)

Have you ever communicated the same point using more than one method or device?

Which brings us to the fraught world of business. It is now customary for professionals to lay their devices on the table before a meeting like gunfighters with revolvers on card tables in saloons. This says to the other people in the room: 'I'm connected. I'm busy. I'm important. If this meeting doesn't hold my interest, I've got lots of other things to do.' According to Jack Trout in *In Search of the Obvious*, this reduces many meetings to little more than gadget envy sessions. Recent research shows that a third of Yahoo staff regularly check email during meetings and 20 per cent of them have been castigated for poor meeting etiquette in this regard.

Many businesses have realized the disadvantage of using email for selling. People now ignore email in the same way that they used to with unsolicited junk mail. Research shows that in any communication, body language accounts for 55 per cent of the power of your message, tone for 38 per cent and words just 7 per cent. So while pinging off rapid messages using text, email or instant messaging increases speed and efficiency, it loses much of the passion, creativity and responsiveness that eye-to-eye or ear-to-ear contact can add. Removing the human can remove the humanity. Judicious use of social media can, however, yield tremendous benefits for companies, if they do it right. Many companies miss the point and try to hijack the online world for broadcast purposes. Peer endorsement and recommendation can be highly powerful, but it is not something that can be manipulated.

Human interaction releases a 'cuddle' chemical called oxytocin. We don't get this if we rely too much on virtual interaction and we risk isolation as a result. Even being present with colleagues while they are clearly not engaged because they are fiddling with some device or other isn't conducive to good work or productive relationships. In Silicon Valley, some tech firms became so exasperated by this problem that they tried introducing 'topless' meetings – as in laptop-less. Computers and BlackBerrys were banned in the hope of making participants concentrate properly on the matter in hand. There was too much resistance and it didn't catch on.

Remember this

Human interaction releases a 'cuddle' chemical called oxytocin. We don't get this if we rely on too much virtual interaction.

If you have found yourself answering 'yes' or 'maybe' to many of the questions in this chapter, then you may well be edicted. Take the test to find out. Then we will move on to a set of ideas to help wean us off our technological drugs and lead a more fulfilling life. We are looking to restore the balance in your life, so that you can make technology work for you and feel that you are getting the best out of it. At the end of each chapter you will find Taming Technology Tips – simple things that you can do to regain control.

Need to tame your technology? Take the test

1 Do you ever interrupt a conversation with your partner or children to take a call?

Never

Occasionally

Off and on

Quite often

Always

2 Have you ever regretted sending a text or email?

Never

Occasionally

Off and on

Quite often

Always

3 Do you check emails for several hours a day?

Never

Occasionally

Off and on

Quite often

Always

4 Do you find yourself distracted by social media sites when you should be doing something else?

Never

Occasionally

Off and on

Quite often

Always

5 Have you ever failed to notice what someone was doing or saying because you were concentrating on your phone or computer?

Never

Occasionally

Off and on

Quite often

Always

6 Have you ever become deeply angry and frustrated by technology?

Never

Occasionally

Off and on

Quite often

Always

7 Have you ever used technology to avoid talking face-to-face?

Never

Occasionally

Off and on

Quite often

Always

8 Have you ever communicated the same point using more than one method or device?

Never

Occasionally

Off and on

Quite often

Always

9 Does your desire to stay in the loop distract you from the people who matter most?

Never

Occasionally

Off and on

Quite often

Always

10 Have you ever been the victim of an online scam?

Never

Occasionally

Off and on

Quite often

Always

Scoring

Give yourself 5 for each 'Always' answer.

Give yourself 4 for each 'Quite often' answer.

Give yourself 3 for each 'Off and on' answer.

Give yourself 2 for each 'Occasionally' answer.

Give yourself 1 for each 'Never' answer.

What your score means

If you scored 10–20, you are not edicted and have superb willpower. Throw this book away or give it to a friend who needs it.

If you scored 21–30, you are fairly under the cosh, so you should definitely read on.

If you scored 31–40, you are definitely edicted but you can pull out of it. Read on, look hard at the Taming Technology Tips and start making some changes as soon as possible.

If you scored, 41–50, it's amazing you've had the time to read this far, considering the amount of time you spend using technology. You are very edicted and definitely need to try everything this book suggests, or call a doctor.

Focus points

✵ Your phone and other devices only interrupt you if they are turned on. The number of interruptions you receive has a direct bearing on what you can achieve. If you are generally interrupted more often than you would like, then you need to change something.

✵ Email volumes are very much on the increase but what conversations are we having? Personal email needs control when it comes to spam and eating into family time. Work email can be all-consuming and in many jobs it is now impossible to answer the number of inbound messages in a working day.

* Distraction or action? It takes around 15 minutes to get back to your original task when you are interrupted, so technological interventions can have a huge bearing on your ability to get stuff done.

* Hiding behind technology is not good. Important and sensitive conversations need to be had in person. It doesn't pay to use the wrong medium for a conversation that requires careful attention.

* Look at your test results to establish your level of technological dependency. Then move on to look at the steps you can take to offset the influence that it currently has on your life.

Next step

Chapter 3 explains the importance of creating proper time to think, usually by removing yourself from technological distractions.

Thinking

In this chapter you will learn:

▶ *How powerful thinking is: we could dictate our own lives, if only we thought first.*

▶ *Small thoughts are as valuable as big ones, and often easier and less daunting to implement.*

▶ *In order to think properly we need to remove ourselves from incessant distractions. That means turning off our technological devices for a time.*

▶ *That taking control, facing up to our failings and accepting responsibility for our actions can be life-changing. Often for the better.*

▶ *To take some time to ponder. You could make better decisions as a result.*

Thinking, talking, communicating, doing and being

So it's time to tame your technology and get your life back. Whether you are totally ruled by machines or just feeling the tide turning against you, now is the time to act and regain control. It's time to confront the problem and make some resolutions that change things for the better. There are five main areas that require attention: thinking, talking, communicating, doing and being. They are all interrelated but are worth breaking down so that we can concentrate harder on what they mean and how they can affect our relationship with technology. We will devote a chapter to each, but first, a quick overview of how they work.

Thinking. We don't do enough of it, even though it's completely free. Events overtake us. We need to rediscover the art of thinking clearly and use it to improve our quality of life.

Thinking takes time and requires a bit of peace and quiet. We can't think properly if we are distracted and distraction comes in lots of ways. If you are trying to think and you are constantly interrupted by inbound alerts, you may never crack the problem. So it doesn't work if the phone keeps going, or an email, text or instant message comes in, or if we are trying to multitask and not making a good job of it. So we need to create the time and space to get away from technology at certain times to think properly.

Talking. We do too much of it, often without having thought first. We talk too much rubbish and not enough sense. It's time for a new, more considered approach that reflects what we feel more accurately and makes it easier for others to understand us.

If we don't think then there is a very strong chance that the quality of our talk will suffer. This works in two directions. Firstly, people who don't think first tend to talk nonsense in any medium. Secondly, the person who has to listen to the resulting drivel is either frustrated or hasn't a clue what the other person is talking about. Neither state of affairs is good. People who blurt out any old rubbish without thinking create the impression that they don't think much (which could be true), and are also lousy communicators, so nobody wins. Many claim that they can't work out what they think until they talk it through. This may be true, but at least they should have the courtesy to alert the other person that that is what they are about to do. The recipient of the outburst (the wafflee) has the right to know what they are in for (from the waffler). Talking straight affects how well you can communicate through your technology.

Communicating. *We have so many methods of communicating available to us that we frequently choose the wrong one. We need the right medium for the right message and a clear understanding of the suitability of each for the task.*

Communicating is a broader skill. It includes talking of course, but also embraces many other media, such as the phone, email, text, instant messaging, social media, presentations and much more. Communication is two-way, and can rarely be achieved by a monologue, unless you happen to be the president making a speech – and even then there is plenty of room for misunderstanding. This means that listening is a crucial part of communicating if it is to be successful. Choosing the right medium is absolutely critical. How many times have you chosen the wrong medium for the message? It happens all the time, and the more technological options we have, the more baffling it becomes.

Doing. *We do far too much of the wrong stuff, which often means we do not have enough time left for the right stuff. We need to be able to distinguish between what matters and what doesn't to make better use of our time.*

Doing is the action part. Without it, nothing happens. Writers do not sit waiting for inspiration to strike. They sit and write until something emerges. Anyone can have a great idea but it is worth nothing unless it gets done. In that respect, execution has become one of the most valuable traits in the modern world. People mistakenly think of execution as the tactical side or menial side of things. They couldn't be more wrong. People who get seduced into concentrating on the so-called 'bigger picture' usually fail to deliver. In 2000, 40 of the top Fortune 200 company chief executives were dismissed because their organizations had failed to do what they promised. There should never be a gap between thinking and doing. Technology can fool people into thinking that something is being done when in fact it isn't, as we shall see.

Being. We can all be better. We should define our own characters, not allow them to be defined by our possessions or technology. Having a better life starts with knowing what you are all about and emanating that style.

And finally, being. Existence, and the quality of it, is the very essence of life. So it must be worth making sure that what we are suits us well. Our self-determination and self-esteem may well be enhanced by technology, but they certainly should not be ruled by it. Getting your attitude to your technology right and having a decent balance leads to less stress and a more fulfilled life. It starts with good thinking, emerges as well-considered talking and communicating, and manifests itself as doing, which leads to high-quality being. And if you believe the words of Rene Descartes – 'I think, therefore I am' – then the cycle from thinking to being is complete.

Mind games

Thinking is the essence of a decent life. The more people do it, the more fun and fulfilment they have. Everything that gives us pleasure involves a thought – generous deeds, great design, fantastic entertainment, everything. Someone somewhere thought carefully about how something could be, and then they crafted it and made it exist. We can't all be inventors and master craftsmen, but we can pause for a while and make our own little sphere of influence that little bit better. Thinking is how we bear responsibility. Without it we don't take any and so we relinquish what happens to us and to other people. That's no way to live. If you don't pause to think, you'll be dictated to by everybody else who does. And if you don't pause to think about your technology, then you'll be dictated to by your machines. Life suddenly becomes interesting when you take charge.

As the philosopher John Stuart Mill said, 'One person with belief is equal to a force of 99 who have only interests.'

Stimulating thinkers the world over generate the kind of competition that we all cherish and enjoy. Great debating, great sportsmen and women, great chess players – they are all brilliant thinkers. The internet has generated a much bigger forum for the exchange of ideas and views, but it has also created a paradox of choice, as we saw in Chapter 1. Thinking needs to be done in a stimulating environment that suits the thinker, and we can replicate our own modest version of this quality all on our own. It takes some discipline, but it's not really that hard if you concentrate and put your mind to it. Let's break this down into small chunks to make it clearer and probably less daunting.

Starting with the miniscule: would you ever walk into a room without deciding why? Or drink a glass of water without deciding you were thirsty? No you wouldn't. Each action involves an initial thought, however seemingly small or inconsequential. In the next five minutes, you will make many such decisions, and when you add them all up, you'll have filled a day. So, to make today more fruitful, take a minimum of five minutes, but preferably fifteen, to decide how you are going to interact with your technology today and why that is appropriate. Ask yourself: why am I writing this email? Why am I logging on to this social network? Why am I using this machine? If you cannot answer why to your own satisfaction then there may be no value in using it for doing that particular thing.

It is then a simple matter to extend this principle to a month, a year or a lifetime, but of course the longer the time span under consideration, the longer you will need. This is not an anti-technology stance. In fact, technology can enable our ability to think if used thoughtfully. One 83-year-old has made a habit of printing out his social media updates and highlighting those that are not contributing to what he calls a full life. He then ceases engaging in 'unfruitful activities' from then on. We don't do enough thinking, even though it's completely free. Events will always try to overtake us, but we urgently need to rediscover the art of thinking clearly and use it to improve our quality of life.

Thinking is free, so do it more often

How many times have we heard someone say that they haven't had time to think? Millions of people say it every day, but what does it actually mean? If you analyse the phrase carefully, it is complete nonsense. Every sentient being spends the entire day thinking, absorbing circumstances and reacting to them. Of course, the phrase is not literal. What it really means is that they haven't had time to pause and think about the things that really matter, because lots of irrelevant stuff has got in the way. This is a tragedy and it is your job to create the appropriate time to rectify the position.

Remember this

We don't do enough thinking, even though it's completely free.

Why is this so important? Because, although you may claim that you are too busy to create the time, if you haven't worked out whether what you are doing with your technology is the right thing, then you may only be busy pursuing all the wrong things. Never engage with it unless you know why you are doing it. This sounds blindingly obvious and yet most people frequently do things without knowing why.

So now is the time to get thinking. You need to set aside the time and create the appropriate conditions. Some people like total peace and seclusion, others like something to shake them up. Work out your style by considering whether you are more likely to have some decent ideas if you sit on top of a mountain, have a massage, get on the running machine, disappear to a country cottage, drink a bottle of quality wine, leave the country for the day, visit the zoo or go fishing. The activity or circumstance doesn't matter, so long as it is different from where you normally are and what you normally do.

Remove yourself from the persistent attention of your technology, even for an hour, and think. You have to enter the thinking process in the right frame of mind. It's no use being petrified, depressed, cynical, paranoid, resentful, jaded or any other negative emotion. It is okay to be a bit vexed or concerned.

It is all right to be mildly sceptical. It is fine to be quizzical. In fact, that should positively be encouraged. Your objective should be to reflect on how you interact with your machines and view it as though you were someone else looking at you. Strange, and quite detaching, but ultimately rewarding. Write down how long you spend on machines each day. Keep a diary for a week. Survey the results. How do you fare?

Small thoughts are as valuable as big ones

A lot of people get hung up on planning the 'next big thing'. But who is to say that the next big thing has to be big? In technological terms it could be quite small, such as moving your laptop to a different place or adjusting a setting on your mobile. Sometimes tiny increments of change make amazing things happen. As Malcolm Gladwell says in *The Tipping Point*, little things can make a big difference if cunningly applied. So don't panic about the fear that you need to come up with something outstandingly original. People rarely do. Occasionally someone like Edison will invent a light bulb but that's a bit beyond our remit.

Unlock the facts

Sometimes tiny increments of change make amazing things happen.

The architect and furniture designer Ludwig Mies Van Der Rohe once proclaimed that 'God is in the details.' There is often great mileage to be had from lots of little ideas. Little ideas are great. They are less hard to come up with, they are usually cheaper and easier to implement, and they can be done more quickly than something big and scary. This enables you to work out rapidly whether they are any good or not. Little ideas can be test-driven constantly, refined, enlarged, developed or withdrawn with the minimum of fuss. Think hard about your relationship with your technology and try making your next big thing small. You might surprise yourself.

Thinking or just rearranging your prejudices?

William James said that a great many people think they are thinking when they are merely rearranging their prejudices. If everything is too samey, or things aren't going that well, it's time for a re-think. And that does not mean rearranging your prejudices or dreaming up new reasons to prove that you are right about something. It means taking a hard look at what you've got and working out whether it is any good or not and whether you like your circumstances.

Unlock the facts

You need to set aside the time and create appropriate thinking conditions.

If you have any doubts about your approach to technology, a long, hard look is exactly what's needed. Even in the unlikely event that you don't have any concerns at all, it is still a great thing to do. Everything can always be made better or more stimulating. The philosopher Bertrand Russell famously said: 'Many people would sooner die than think. In fact they do.' Make sure you don't die, if only technologically, from a lack of thought. Work hard to clarify your thinking and don't shy from the task. It's your life and you want it back.

Case study: Darren the Digital Guy

Darren was a really bright guy who worked in a social media agency. He was an expert at code and knew his way round the web like no one else. When he was 'in the zone', he could plough through vast amounts of work, hammering away at his keyboard with his headphones on for hours on end. He was usually left alone for extended periods and then as soon as he solved a major problem or invented something brilliant he would be given stacks more to do.

He was well respected by his colleagues, but there was a catch – no one really knew how much work he ever had on, and because his subject matter was quite specialized, there was no manager who really knew what a sensible workload was for someone of his type. So they just kept sending work his way and, because he was essentially a nice guy, he never said no.

Like so many people who find it hard to say no, the motivation for always saying yes came from an intrinsic desire to please everybody. Darren didn't decline tasks because he felt that he would then be seen as lazy or unco-operative. So he just kept taking the projects on and soon the changes to his original (acceptable) work pattern began to kick in.

First to go were the lunch breaks. Some fresh air and a sandwich out of the office became a thing of the past and were gradually replaced by a snack at his desk while still working or no lunch at all. Then the leaving time slid from 6 p.m. to 7 p.m. to 8 p.m. and sometimes later. He started coming in earlier, and when that wasn't enough, he started taking work home with him and carrying on over a bottle of wine in front of the TV in the evenings. Soon that started eating into his weekends and then the inevitable happened – he had to cancel a holiday to meet a supposedly vital deadline.

In all the kick and rush, something important was falling by the wayside. He was getting huge amounts done – there was no doubt about that – but the truth was he never had any time to think properly, so he didn't honestly know if he was busying himself with the right stuff. When he finally got a nasty bout of flu that knocked him out completely for nearly two weeks, he realized it was time to make some changes.

He realized that thinking and doing are not the same thing and too much or too little of either isn't healthy. So he instigated a new regime. Every morning he took 20 minutes to think about the day ahead. This was a regular moment of calm reflection and crucially took place well away from his computer and in the absence of his hand-held device. With a clear head, no interruptions and a small notebook, he could gain a clear perspective on what the day held. He often concluded that several of his tasks were not worth doing at all, and after careful thought he would often go to colleagues and propose a change to what had originally been requested.

Making proper thinking time a part of his routine changed his approach to work.

How to out-think yourself

If you want to out-think yourself, you first need to face up to your failings. The purpose of this is not to beat yourself up but to help you recognize what you tend *not* to do well in relation to your machines. You can then set about working out ways to work around those deficiencies. Mostly, these are just small shortcomings that are mildly irritating, but if you have several deficiencies they can put some fairly large barriers in the way of you thinking clearly. Knowing yourself helps you to address problems and think more productively.

Out-thinking yourself requires that you use your calm, controlled moments in order to anticipate what you will get wrong or fail to do at a later uncontrolled moment. If you often forget your house keys then introduce some changes to counteract the problem. It only takes a minute to dream up some initiatives that might help: put a note on the back of the door to remind yourself, hang them on a hook there, always put them in the same place, keep a spare set at work or with a neighbour, put them in your trousers, briefcase or handbag the night before, and so on.

If you often run out of petrol, you can do the same. Put a note on your steering wheel saying petrol, always fill up on the same day of the week, always fill up when the tank is half full, put a spare can in the boot or buy a bicycle. The knack is to admit at the outset that you will probably not do the job, and then work out the most effective way to make sure that you do. Take one thing at a time and don't try to fix everything at once. The Taming Technology Tips give you lots of ideas about how to apply this to your technology.

Your locus of control

Grabbing control of this whole area and taking responsibility for your actions is what psychologists call your locus of control. Julian Rotter's 'social learning theory' suggests that there are essentially two types of people depending on their upbringing. Those with an internal locus of control believe that reinforcement depends on personal efforts. They think they are in charge of their lives and act accordingly. They are physically and mentally healthier and more socially skilled. Their parents tend to have been supportive, generous with praise, consistent with discipline and non-authoritarian. Those with an external locus of control believe that reinforcement depends on outside sources – so they make fewer attempts to improve their lives and get things done.

Unlock the facts

Those with an internal locus of control believe that they are in charge of their lives and act accordingly.

Clearly you cannot change your upbringing but you can aspire to the qualities represented by an internal locus of control. That means taking responsibility for your technology, recognizing that improvements can be made and acknowledging that it is down to you. It's no good sitting passively claiming that there is nothing you can do, because there is. As Jim Watson points out, 'You can say, "Gee, your life must be pretty bleak if you don't think there's a purpose" but I'm anticipating having a good lunch.'

Turn-on or turn-off?

If the philosopher Bertrand Russell was right that many people would sooner die than think, then we can reasonably assume that a lot of people simply don't like doing it. Not only is this a shame, but also it is totally counterproductive for any individual. Absence of thought effectively cedes decision-making to the random events of life. That abdication of responsibility may well allow the individual to claim that they are a victim of circumstances, but they are wrong to believe it. Being the passive recipient of everyone else's actions is no way to live. As George Bernard Shaw pointed out, progress in the world relies solely on the unreasonable man, who shapes the world rather than allows it to shape him. This is how you should approach your relationship with your technology. Only then will you get your life back.

Unlock the facts

Remove yourself from the persistent attention of your technology and think.

Thinking needs to become a turn-on, not a turn-off. Where technology is concerned, there are two ways to approach this. The first is to deliberately choose a new and stimulating online environment to help your thinking and the second is to turn it all off. Choose the one you prefer or try both. Then when you have the setting you want, you can begin to concentrate on the matter in hand, and, given the frenzied pace of modern life, there may well be many issues to review. The brain is a bundle of bodily tissue and needs exercise like any other. If you don't use it very often, it will hurt like hell when you do. As Barbara Castle once commented: 'If a problem is hard, think, think, then think again. It will hurt at first, but you'll get used to it.' When did you last give yours a really good workout?

The best type of thinking is simple, not complex. Begin with the sort of questions that children might ask. Ask 'Why?' three times in a row to extract a better reason for doing, or not doing, something. Draw up lists of questions and work through them carefully. If you really don't know the answers, then do some research. Learning is discovery. Embrace the art of inquisition. Think about what to say and what *not* to say. Think about which technological medium is the most appropriate in which to say it so that you can express your feelings in a helpful and effective way.

It's time to make some resolutions to start your revolution. Look back at how you fared in the test and consider how much you need to think about your approach to technology. Now think again based on this chapter and consider whether any of the tips can help.

Taming Technology Tips for Thinking

1 Turn off every device and appliance you have to create thinking time

This may sound a bit extreme but it's a great discipline, even if you only ever do it once. You'll probably conclude that there is at least one piece of machinery that you never use anyway and you'll probably reduce your electricity bill.

2 Walk away from your machines and go somewhere quiet

If you really can't unplug the stuff, perhaps if you are at work, then hide yourself away somewhere appropriate. Don't tell anybody where you are. Enjoy the silence and really think. It will hurt at first but you'll get used to it. Do not take your mobile phone with you – it is not your Siamese twin. The world will not fall apart if you cannot be contacted for a short while, but *you* might fall apart if you can be reached every moment of the day.

3 Try creating some online thinking time

Choose a totally new online environment – one that you never normally use or engage with. This could be a new world of music, film, photography or writing. Use that stimulus to push your ideas to new places. A word of warning though – don't use this approach as simply another excuse to spend ages sitting at a computer. Concentrate on the mental stimulation it offers, not the act of sitting in front of a monitor.

4 Use something simple like a pen and paper to note any good thoughts

It's refreshing to use a different medium, particularly if you spend a lot of time tapping away on a keyboard. You might even sketch some pictures or diagrams. You will probably also find that you express your ideas differently. There is nothing that says that your ideas should be expressed through a keyboard, and many now lament the reduction in handwriting skills that has resulted.

5 Review your day, week month or year

The longer the period in question, the more thinking time you will need. Choose your medium and your time period. Think about what you feel you have to do and compare it with what you really *want* to do. If there is a significant difference between the two, work out what needs to change, pledge to change it and write it down.

6 Move your technology to give you more peace

Your approach to your technology could change depending on where it is. If you are constantly tempted to log on or generally fiddle, then move that device into another room and keep it there. For mobile devices, put them as far away as possible when you need to think. Get into a habit that forces you to actively decide to interact with a machine, rather than have it interrupt you. A person I trained recently decided to put a plastic bag over his second monitor to reduce his distraction levels.

7 Remove alerts on all computers and devices

If you react like Pavlov's dog whenever your computer or hand-held device makes a noise, then turn these alerts off. *You* decide when and for what period of time you wish to interact with them, not the other way round. Anyone with obsessive mobile disorder needs to break the pattern. Don't be a lapdog to your laptop.

8 Always turn your phone off when you want to think

Honestly, you can wait a few minutes for a message, and bear in mind that seeing or hearing what the other person has to say, and having an extra moment to think about it, may alter or improve your response. So you will also gain another type of thinking time. Someone I was in a meeting with had seven 'urgent' voice mails and 100 emails on his phone after our meeting. I was very pleased he didn't have it on while we were chatting.

9 Design a regime for the only times you will look at your devices

Once in the morning, once at lunchtime and once at the end of the day. That should be enough. If you feel it isn't, then do ask yourself when you are going to get anything done. Carve the day up into chunks and choose when you will do things on *your* terms rather than simply deal with everyone else's requests. This is also part of you educating everyone else with regard to when it suits you to interact with them.

10 Make thinking time a part of your routine

Once you are sold on the idea, thinking should become an integral part of your day, week or month. Grab your diary now and map out times when you actively want to think. Fifteen minutes each morning, an hour at the beginning or end of each week, a day a month, or a week a year are suggested amounts for you to consider. It's time to regain control.

Focus points

* Thinking is free, so do it more often. Too many people claim that they don't have time to think, but this is very much to their detriment. Force an initiative in your daily or weekly routine to allow yourself time to ponder. You will make better decisions as a result, especially in relation to your technology.

* Small thoughts are as valuable as big ones. Don't get hung up on 'the big idea'. Lots of smaller initiatives are easier to experiment with. They take less effort to implement and they can be withdrawn fast if they don't work.

* Work out how to out-think yourself. If you are persistently poor at something, then come up with some interventions that improve matters. You don't want to be sitting in a retirement home saying you were never any good at something.

* If you want to think properly, turn off your technological devices or go somewhere where there aren't any. It's a rare moment in modern life when you can really get some peace and mull things over. If you can engineer this into your work routine, you'll make better decisions and proceed in a much calmer way.

* Try some of the Taming Technology Tips for Thinking. Start with one or two. If they work, keep going. If they don't, try some others.

Next step

Chapter 4 identifies the link between clear thought and clear speech and explains how technology can help or hinder clarity.

4

Talking

In this chapter you will learn:

▶ *The value of thinking before you speak. Brevity equals intelligence.*

▶ *The benefit of talking straight and how to do it. If people understand what you are saying, they can do what you're asking.*

▶ *How to listen properly and how to avoid people waffling at you. Give someone the purity of your attention, but ensure that they are straight-talking.*

▶ *How to say 'No' politely. People who say yes too much pile pressure on themselves and may end up letting themselves, and others, down. Get your life back.*

▶ *Does your point pass the 'grandmother test'? Can you explain what you're thinking simply and concisely so a lay-person could understand?*

The art of brachylogy

Brachylogy. It's an odd word but one really worth considering. It means a concise style in speech or writing. Making something pithy is far harder than rambling on, as all wafflers know. As Blaise Pascal, the scientist and philosopher who lived in the 1600s, once pointed out, 'I have made this longer than usual because I did not have time to make it shorter.' (This saying is sometimes attributed to Mark Twain, but Pascal certainly came first). It sounds contradictory, but it isn't. Anyone can drone on for a long time, but thoughtful people think about what they are going to say first, then they say it. And when they do, it's usually worth listening to. So let's look at how we can talk more succinctly with our machines and so free up time to work more effectively with them or do something else.

Brevity equals intelligence. The prevailing mood of much modern speech is long-winded, circuitous and not necessarily very well thought out. You only have to listen to a politician to hear that. You should always aim to *talk straight* – to construct clear, jargon-free sentences and say them out loud. Many find this difficult but with concentration it should be within everybody's grasp. The clarity of your spoken approach will be a direct reflection of your clarity of thought and will have a huge bearing on your use of, and power over, your technology. Using speech correctly should reduce the amount of time you spend using machines, especially phones.

Unlock the facts
Brevity equals intelligence.

The less time it takes to articulate a point, the better expressed it is. The more you leave out, the closer you get to the heart of the matter. Your first instinct of what to say may well include all sorts of broad material but it is not until careful thought is applied to the main point that much of it can be discarded. More material does not necessarily strengthen an argument or improve clarity. In some complex academic and technical areas it might, but in most areas of life, it doesn't. Skilful editing and the ability to filter out extraneous material is a crucial asset for anyone who wants to tame their technology effectively.

You will probably have heard the expression that **less is more**. This is the notion that simplicity and clarity lead to good design. It is a phrase often associated with Ludwig Mies Van Der Rohe, one of the founders of modern architecture and a proponent of simplicity of style. Less really *is* more. We talk too much, often without having thought first. We talk too much rubbish and not enough sense. It's time for a new, more considered approach that reflects what we feel more accurately and makes it easier for others to understand us. Brachylogy is the key to using technology.

Thinking and talking straight

The link between thinking straight and talking straight needs to be established in your mind. Pay attention to the connection and consider the consequences of talking twaddle. You can't talk straight if you can't think straight, and translating straight thinking into straight talking pays tremendous dividends. The pitfalls shouldn't need articulating. If someone doesn't talk straight socially, then their friends cannot react specifically. If a person doesn't talk straight in a relationship, then their partner will most likely miss the point. If a parent doesn't talk straight, the child will be confused. If the child doesn't talk straight, then the parent is none the wiser. If a boss doesn't talk straight, then his or her staff cannot take suitable action. If staff don't talk straight, then the boss is misinformed and cannot take appropriate action. It's a nasty chain of confusion that usually triggers the need for further action unnecessarily.

Talking straight is a vital component of clear communication and is crucial to the speed and efficacy with which things get done. This has an immediate bearing on whether you will then have to interact with technology or not. If a thought, request or instruction is unclear, then there is a strong chance that there will have to be another conversation, and that probably means another phone call, email, text or instant message. Or several of these. Or a mixture of all of them. In a work context this could get even worse, since it may well generate the need for a re-draft or a whole new proposal. It all means extra work, and more time on a computer, with a phone nailed to your ear or fiddling with a device. It's better to get it right first time.

Unlock the facts

Talking properly provides a crucial bridge between thinking and communicating.

The best communicators understand how language works and concentrate hard on it. The great thing about concentrating on how language works is that you gain two fundamental benefits:

1 You can talk straight yourself.

2 You can identify when some one else is not talking straight.

Guidance on how to talk straight is all around us. Good books, talk radio shows, great speakers, and, of course, the dictionary are all sources of learning and should be consulted frequently. Inquisitive students of language should try to look at a dictionary every day. Try to understand the correct definitions of figures of speech and use them appropriately. When used in the right context, they can enhance communication and understanding and enrich your life. If people understand you better, then there will be less confusion and therefore less stress. It starts in your head and it's your job to explain it to the rest of the world clearly via your machines.

Spotting waffle

There are two types of waffle: internal and external. Internal waffle is talking rubbish to yourself. It sounds near impossible but millions of people do it. You can just hear the words, unspoken, rattling around in their heads as they embark on a marathon bout of self-delusion. It's insidious stuff and arguably even more potent when unsaid than when uttered out loud. Internal wafflers believe their own propaganda and base decisions on it – often important ones. They then regurgitate their muddled thinking through their technology as observations and requests to others, usually causing chaos and confusion in the process and generating the need for more and more exchanges.

It is beyond doubt that we live in a tricky verbal world. What can you do about it? Here is a ten-point guide to spotting deceptive waffle. Remember: a lot of the language is very hard to penetrate, so you need to listen hard and question very deeply. Check any statement or request for action for the following:

1 **False arguments** If you know your facts and the other person is incorrect, then you should either ignore them or refuse to act on their instructions. In fact, you may not even be able to do so.

2 **Circular arguments** If the person in question keeps returning to the same point, then there may only be one point. If it's valid, then fine. If it's not, ignore it or do not act on it.

3 **Repetition** Similar to the circular argument, but not quite the same. In the circular example, the speaker will head off elsewhere and then return. In the case of repetition, they just keep saying the same thing, albeit using different words.

4 **Incorrect conclusions** These are 'synapse jumps' and what the Romans called a *non sequitur*. The synapse is the point at which a nerve impulse is relayed from the terminal portion of an axon to the dendrites of an adjacent neuron. The charge jumps the gap to let your brain know what's going on. People often jump a gap and end up in completely the wrong place. A *non sequitur* is just that: a statement that has little or no relevance to what preceded it – literally 'it does not follow'.

5 **Spurious sources** Some people make themselves sound authentic by quoting sources, but they may not be valid. Check these assertions carefully and question them closely.

6 **Irrelevance** It is extraordinary the amount of irrelevant material that is wheeled out to validate a point. In fact, the more evidence is offered, the more inquisitive you might wish to be – the 'Thou doth protest too much' syndrome.

7 **Weak points** Most decent cases either argue for themselves or have one or two solid support points. If someone puts up a chart with support points, the weak points at the bottom always undermine the strong points at the beginning. If this is the case, review the entire argument.

8 **Cliché and jargon** Don't trust it. It is usually disguising something.

9 **Inconsistency** Inconsistency is to be viewed suspiciously if it appears in the same burst of speech. But also keep an eye out for it over time. Many people contradict themselves in subsequent statements.

10 **Vagueness** Vagueness should be easy to spot. If the person can't come to the point, or clearly hasn't got one, then ignore them or don't do what they say.

By learning to spot all this, and by not doing it yourself, you will automatically be talking straight and so reducing the amount of repeat tasks that will force you to engage with technology unnecessarily.

The spontaneous word dump

One of the worst examples of bad talking is the spontaneous word dump. This takes many forms. Any of your machines could burst into life at any time and suddenly there someone is, talking to you. It could be your phone, in which case the caller may or may not ask whether this is a convenient time for you, and in our time-pressed world, it very rarely is. It might be a text, an instant message or an email. All were originally designed for brief notifications or exchanges of information but have now morphed into just more media for extended diatribes. Or you may be at work and hear the dreaded words: 'Have you got a minute?' Whether you are at your desk concentrating on a task, or on your way to somewhere and subject to the 'corridor surprise', chances are you *haven't* got a minute, but the person is going to start talking anyway.

> ### Remember this
> We talk too much, often without thinking first.

The spontaneous word dump is one of the most thoughtless acts a human being can perpetrate on another. It gives the other person no warning, pays no regard to whether it is convenient for them and is totally selfish. It is intended solely to benefit the dumper, not the dumpee. Regular dumpers use more and more cunning ways to dump and technology is their unwitting accomplice. People who receive too many phone calls eventually stop answering. People who are intercepted in the corridor one too many times can barely make it to the washrooms in time. One beleaguered executive complained that whenever she left her desk, a phalanx of hangers-on and questioners used to form behind her as though she were the Pied Piper of Hamelin. If you are a spontaneous dumper, it is time to take stock and realize what a monumental waste of time it is. No one wins if everybody is speaking before they think, except possibly the phone companies.

How to listen properly

Conversations should be two-way, so they should be equal. This vests responsibility in both parties. It is the duty of the speaker to speak clearly and concisely having thought carefully about what they wish to say, and it is the role of the other person to listen properly. Listening is a dying art. It has been said that there are no conversations any more, just intersecting monologues. Martin Lomasney pointed out that you should: 'Never write when you can speak. Never speak when you can nod.'

Listening is a skill. Ernest Hemingway said: 'I like to listen. I have learned a great deal from listening carefully. Most people never listen.' And Doug Larson said that, 'wisdom is the reward you get for a lifetime of listening when you'd have preferred to talk.'

Unlock the facts

'Wisdom is the reward you get for a lifetime of listening when you'd have preferred to talk.'

The greatest gift you can give another person is the purity of your attention. So next time someone talks to you, listen properly, particularly if you are using aural technology. Start by saying nothing. Let the words roll over you, take it in and try to understand. Then when there is a pause, offer your opinion. There is a catch though. If they are a waffler, then this approach might drive you mad. As we have seen, a conversation bears a two-way responsibility. If you are the regular recipient of a deluge of monologue, then you may need to have a word with the habitual waffler or dream up some containment strategies. These can be devious or pragmatic and need to be judged depending on the context. Getting away from the source of the waffle may be essential. Here are some suggestions for escape lines:

▶ I am late for a meeting. Can we pursue this later?

▶ I am right on a deadline. Can we pursue this later?

▶ I've just remembered something important. Can we pursue this later?

▶ Can you talk to a colleague about it?

▶ Can I talk to a colleague about it?

▶ Will you excuse me? I need to have a quick word with someone.

▶ Will you excuse me for a moment? I need to go to the bathroom.

Case study: Caroline the Waffler

Caroline was a waffler and secretly she knew it. She was one of those people who never sat quietly and thought something through or committed her thoughts to paper. Instead, she would collar the nearest person and just start talking, regardless of what words came out of her mouth. After several months of this it was annoying a fair number of her colleagues, so her boss took her aside to talk to her about it.

'Let's have a chat about these spontaneous outbursts, why you do them and the effect it has on your colleagues,' said her boss Stephanie. 'First of all, can you explain why you need to prevail on others like this?'

'Well,' said Caroline, not entirely surprised, 'I find it hard to articulate what I want to say without running it by someone else first. If I have a half-baked idea, then I can usually finesse it if I test-drive it on someone else.'

'Fair enough,' said Stephanie, 'but people say that often you ambush them from behind a pillar in the corridor when they are on the way to the loo and least expecting it. Do you think that's reasonable?'

'Well I don't intend to specifically, but when I have a thought I need to get it out straightaway.'

'Fair enough, but do you ever ask the other person if it's a convenient moment for them? The word is, you usually start by asking "Have you got a minute?" and then just carry on regardless of whether they have had time to say no or even reply at all.'

'Ah,' said Caroline, beginning to see the error of her ways.

'It's not that it's bad to discuss things with your colleagues.' continued Stephanie, 'quite the opposite, in fact – but at the very least it would be polite if you asked them when is convenient for them to listen to your rough ideas, so then it's a fairer interaction. As a matter of interest, how long might such a conversation last?'

'Five minutes?' said Caroline, not entirely convincingly. 'Well, fifteen or twenty sometimes – now that I think of it.'

'Well there you go,' said Stephanie. 'That's a lot of time to rip out of someone's day, especially if they didn't even know it was going to happen. And what do you think would happen if all 200 people in the company did that?'

'Mmm, we wouldn't get much done,' admitted Caroline. 'I need to think more carefully about the effect on the wafflee.'

'The wafflee?'

'Yes – the person who has to listen to me waffling. I need to be more considerate instead of just prevailing on them whenever I happen to be in the mood to try out an idea.'

'That's it,' concluded Stephanie, pleased at Caroline's moment of self-realization.

Caroline wasn't upset. She knew very well that she was a waffler. She decided to make a personal pledge about how to control her waffling tendencies in the future. Step one was to think more carefully before she spoke, always pausing to check that her ideas were as developed as they possibly could be before exposing them to someone else. Step two was to ask the other person when was a convenient time to try out a new idea and ask how long they had to listen to it. Then her conversations would neither be a surprise to the other person nor unwelcome.

How to say no politely

Another use of talk to get your life back is to say no more often. It sounds a bit blunt but it can be done politely as we shall see. These suggestions have to be handled sensitively. Your ability to use them will depend hugely on your level of experience, the quality of your relationship with the person you are talking to and the tone you adopt. There are lots of ways to say no but it is important to realize that aggression never works. Genuine concern to get it right usually does. Bluntly refusing to do something without offering any alternative isn't going to get you very far. But you should become much more inquisitive so that you don't blindly accept whatever you are told to do without believing it to be a good and useful action.

One of the most interesting aspects of saying no politely is that most of the approaches do not actually involve using the word no. Instead the responder listens to the request and probes further, most often suggesting a better line of enquiry or way of solving the issue. In this respect, there is certainly nothing rude or obstructive about questioning the appropriateness of the request – if anything, the new line of enquiry confirms that you have been listening carefully and are genuinely concerned with the outcome. Here are some ways to say no politely that can be applied through a variety of machines.

'The consequences of doing what you suggest are x and y (something not good or helpful). *Are you still sure about this?'*
Let them consider and give them time to think. They may well withdraw the idea once they have heard your opinion. This can be particularly helpful if the person in question respects your opinion.

'I really wouldn't recommend this. It goes against all my previous experience.'
Obviously you need to be reasonably experienced to pull this one off, but it does work when you know that you are respected by the other person and is particularly important if you are part of a team.

'I really don't agree because of reasons x, y, z.'
This is a purely rational response and can be deployed when you have a good understanding of a subject and all the issues. Try to keep it unemotional and let the facts speak for themselves. If they are sufficiently strong then you won't have to push the point.

'May I discuss this with someone else and call you back?'
This is admittedly a case of stalling for time, but it is valid. Many people who ask for something either forget or change their mind by the following day. By building in thinking time, you take the edge off confrontation and allow for a more considered response later.

'I have already discussed that possibility and rejected it as inappropriate for the following reasons.'
A lot of people are very inconsistent. Sometimes a new request flies in the face of what has been discussed before and it is often appropriate to remind them of important discussions that have already taken place. Recap on any previous conversations, meetings and discussions that have a bearing on the outcome.

'I want this to be really carefully thought through. Can I think about it and discuss it with you tomorrow?'

In many walks of life, a solution that takes longer is valued more, whereas the immediate response is regarded as too spontaneous to be well considered. If this is true in a particular circumstance, then you need to understand the value of retiring to think. It also buys you some time and gives you the chance to seek advice if you want to.

'It would be really helpful to understand what has changed because we agreed this yesterday.'

It is amazing the number of times when you think something is agreed and then suddenly it isn't. Even stranger, the person delivering the news often makes no mention of what has changed and what the reasons are. In these circumstances, it is your job to ask the question. It is only reasonable that if you are being asked to do something new you should be told why. If you disapprove of the new direction, then say: *'Mmm, this sheds a different light on things. May I have time to consider?'*

'I can't do all of that, but I might be able to help with some of it.'

Split the problem into parts and offer to solve some of them, but not all of them. This approach allows you to be helpful and responsive without taking on masses of extra things to do. It also gives you the chance to cherry-pick the bits that you are best at or enjoy most.

There are also plenty of rather more devious approaches to saying no. I don't necessarily approve but they can be amusing. Here are my favourites:

▶ Confuse the issue by continually introducing new considerations until they have forgotten their original request.

▶ Say yes. Then find a way of saying no later.

Time for a new language

It's time for a new language – one that understands the link between the brain and the tongue; one that respects the engagement of the one before the deployment of the other; and one that makes best use of what technology can facilitate.

Einstein famously remarked that you do not really understand something until you can explain it to your grandmother, and it's true. The best way to determine whether you are talking straight is to try it out on your mum, your grandmother or a mate in the pub. If they don't understand what you are talking about, then it's too complicated, inconsistent or simply not expressed well enough. And it will be even more prone to misunderstanding over the phone, text, instant message or email.

The mate, mum or grandmother test can also work remotely. Even if they can't be there in person, imagine whether they would know what you were talking about. Would they understand it? If no, then change it. Does it sound daft? If so, then change it. Do you feel stupid when you hear the words out loud? If yes, then change it. Practice regularly how to speak concisely and clearly.

If you want to tame technology and get your life back, talking properly provides a crucial bridge between thinking and communicating. It is a form of communication in its own right and determines whether you need to use another medium. If you can use words to achieve the job on hand, then do it. That's your first port of call. If it were possible to ditch every email and phone call, and conduct all your affairs face-to-face, then most people would. That's not how the world works, but it is the place to start. So before you dive into another round of emails, consider whether you could achieve what you want by chatting to people instead.

Talk takes many forms. If you can't talk directly, then consider meeting up if it's not immediately urgent. If not, then calling is better than email, so put in the effort. So are video conferencing and webinars, because at least they can convey the body language and eye contact that play such a large part in effective communication. Your voice contains subtlety of tone and nuance that the written word never can. That's the sequence: talk in person, replicate the conditions of a face-to-face meeting using technology, speak on the phone, then only email, text or instant message as a last resort.

If you follow this simple sequence, then a number of helpful things will happen. Firstly, you will have more proper direct conversations with people, which will enrich your life, whether socially or at work. You will learn more, enhance your relationships and smooth out many issues more easily and quickly. Crucially, note that a face-to-face conversation involves no technology whatsoever. Secondly, you will make and receive fewer phone calls, because more of your conversations will be direct and personal. That will reduce the number of hours you spend on the phone, and the size of your bill. Thirdly, you will send and receive fewer emails, texts and instant messages. You will also become better at talking.

Taming Technology Tips for Talking

1 **Don't start talking until you have finished thinking**

Think at the beginning of the day about what you will be discussing and work out what you think before you dive in. Concentrate on conversations and subject matter, not on types of technology that can transmit information. If you are caught on the hop, take a second or two to think before you start answering or ask for time to consider. We live in an on-demand world but that doesn't mean that the first thing you think of is the most helpful. Develop the knack of asking for just a little more time so that you can give a more informed response.

2 **Talk straight based on straight thinking**

Consider how you are going to phrase things. Work out a logic chain that explains how you got from A to B and arrived at your point of view. Rehearse how you are going to start and finish what you are going to say and which technology to use. If you are not yet clear about your thinking, then delay your response until you are – there's no point in cobbling something together if it's muddled. A poorly thought out (albeit probably fast) answer will do you no favours.

3 **Be concise, don't waffle and stick to the point**

If you are a self-confessed waffler, then make every effort to stop doing it. Focus your point of view before opening your mouth. Look for synapse jumps that don't make sense and repair the disconnects. Say your piece, then shut up. Practice refining your point into something sharp and clear. Think carefully about vocabulary and phraseology. Rehearse this if you can. Try saying it out loud to see what it sounds like. If it sounds weak, change it before you respond formally.

4 Have the confidence to believe that brevity equals intelligence

The shorter the better. The more you have thought about it, the less time it will take to say. Don't protest too much. Intelligent, confident people can express things fast and clearly without any unnecessary baggage. As soon as you have a line of argument, try it out on someone or test-drive it first. Then work out what you can remove to make it clearer.

5 Learn how to spot waffle and develop skills to deal with it

If you are the wafflee on the receiving end, work hard on coping strategies. Regard it as your job to educate the waffler and control their ramblings. Conversations are two-way and you need to live up to your responsibilities. If somebody starts waffling when you weren't expecting it, nip it in the bud immediately and tell them how long you've got or when is a convenient time.

6 Don't generate spontaneous word dumps

Never ambush someone else with a random piece of nonsense, whether using technology or in person. It's rude and unproductive. Curb your instinct to blurt things out. Pause and come up with something more measured. You will increase your confidence and come across as more intelligent. If you feel compelled to test unformulated thinking on someone else, then at least warn them about it first. Ask when is convenient and how long they have got. Then tailor your thoughts around what suits them – it's only polite.

7 Work hard to develop your listening skills

It's harder than it sounds but it's worth it. Try saying nothing for a while – you might learn something. The wisest, best-informed people listen the most. In particular, practise this on the phone. Most solutions to tricky problems are already lurking in what the originator has to say. Resist the temptation to dive in. Be patient and develop the knack of summarizing effectively – it's a skill that the other person will appreciate.

8 Learn how to say no politely

There are lots of ways to do it, and it doesn't have to be rude. People who say yes too much pile pressure on themselves and may end up letting themselves, and others, down. Saying no will reduce the total amount of things you have to do, the number of interactions with machines and will allow you to concentrate more on what you like doing. You can 'say no' to a piece of technology just as easily as to a person. Develop ways to resist interaction with machines and choose how you want to spend your time.

9 **Study how language works and learn as much as you can**
Look at the dictionary regularly. Listen to great speakers. Read interesting books. Soak up the way words work. It will improve your word power and increase confidence. The more effective direct conversations you have, the less you will have to use technology. It will also inform your choice of technology or the medium. Different messages suit different methods.

10 **Use the mate, mum or grandmother test**
Test-drive what you have to say on someone who knows nothing about it and doesn't care about it. If they don't get it, then you are not talking clearly enough. Start again, improve what you have to say and then choose the most appropriate method with which to say it.

Focus points

✻ Thinking and talking straight are directly linked. Don't blindly dive in to the nearest piece of technology and start talking. You'll probably annoy someone and not express yourself particularly well. Pause to work out what you want to say, then choose your method.

✻ Spotting waffle is a crucial skill in your defence against time-wasting. It can come over the phone or form the main part of a long email. When this happens regularly, it pays to work out what type of waffle is being deployed. This gives you a better chance of coping with it or working out how to fend it off.

✻ How to listen properly is a great skill. It takes patience and preferably at least some interest in the topic or the person talking. Take your time and develop the knack of summarizing what you hear succinctly.

✻ Learning how to say no politely is vital. You can't do everything you are asked to do. Although many people's first instinct is that saying no is rude, in fact it isn't. Most ways of deflecting requests do not actually feature the word 'no' and often lead to a better answer through further discussion.

✻ Try some of the Taming Technology Tips for Talking. Start with one or two. If they work, keep going. If they don't, try some others.

→ Next step

Chapter 5 looks at choosing the right medium for the message to generate clear communication regardless of what technology you are using.

Communicating

In this chapter you will learn:

▶ *That you can't handle it all at once. There is a limit to the number of messages someone can deal with in one day.*

▶ *How to choose the right medium for the right message. Do you understand the suitability of each for the task you have to do?*

▶ *How to write concisely and clearly. If you have to write something, make sure it holds the attention of the reader and says what you intend it to say.*

▶ *Do you HAVE to use technology to communicate? Can you meet, call or write instead?*

▶ *If an email, text or instant message conversation is getting out of hand, stop.*

The death of human interaction?

We have so many methods of communication available to us that not only do we frequently choose the wrong one, but also we often select a method before we have worked out whether that's the best way or not. Talking direct is always best, so everything else is a poor cousin, unless the message warrants nothing more than a quick exchange of information. It is important to remind ourselves that no particular technology is bad as such. It is our lack of thought in using the right type for the job that can be the problem. Documents can remove character from a line of argument. Slides, if not well chosen, can detract from a presentation, and text and email can be the death of conversation.

It is easy to make email the whipping boy here, so let's put it in context. It's about volume and suitability. Those who receive too many emails put in deflective mechanisms. When John Freeman, author of *The Tyranny of Email*, started receiving more than 200 emails a day he knew things needed to change. Do the calculation and you will see that even if he spent just one minute reading and answering each one, it would take him three hours and twenty minutes a day. This is a clear case for taming technology and reclaiming his life back. This sort of volume is probably more common in a work context, but the principle still applies. Some executives are now receiving 100 emails an hour.

Suitability is the second point. Nobody should send an email just because they can. As Stephen Fry said, 'The email of the species is deadlier than the mail.' The medium of email is deficient in relation to talking in person. Entire companies have lost their soul by using the medium and nothing else. In training, I ask who has the most emails in their inbox. Five or six years ago the worst offenders had two or three thousand. The figure has steadily grown to the point where 25,000 is not uncommon. This year the record was smashed by someone who showed me their inbox total of 60,000.

Unlock the facts

The primary benefit of the hand-held device is to boost the self-esteem of the owner.

Those who operate in this way are certainly edicted and are probably technoholics. They are missing out on thousands of opportunities to engage properly with friends and colleagues, and may even be losing the art of doing so. Staff become ostracized from each other as a result. In one company I trained that had 250 staff, such a problem was identified and a new rule was introduced banning internal email on a Friday. Anyone sending one would pay £1 into the charity fund. One employee ended up paying £100. He simply couldn't stop.

Human interaction lies at the heart of a fulfilled life and should be cherished and practised. If the volume of technological interaction has reached silly levels, we need to get our lives back. If our ability to choose the right medium for the message is often found wanting, then we need to think more carefully before communicating with the wrong method. Both are infinitely achievable if we pause and take stock. There are fifty or so ideas in this chapter to help.

Room to hide

One of the questions in the test was: *Have you ever used technology to avoid talking face-to-face?* We know that technology has played a part in what many believe to be a decline in social skills, although it has helped in many others. Some people actively hide behind technology, and this is where the trouble starts. Before email was invented, the old office technique was to take a document, add an instruction to it and put it on someone else's desk. Suddenly, it's not your problem. People do this with email all the time.

Hiding behind technology covers a broad spectrum but falls into three main areas: indecisiveness, ego and cowardice. Let's start at the harmless but nonetheless annoying end. If you want to fix something fast on email, then a specific proposal that requires a decisive answer is vital. So, 'Shall we meet up sometime?' is hopeless, and will simply start a tedious trail of permutations whereas 'Shall we meet? I can do Thursday at 2 or 4, or Friday at 10. Choose one.' demands a clear and decisive response. One can immediately see that the onus is on the person starting the conversation to frame it correctly. This form of hiding is irritating and a waste of time, but not the end of the world.

Next up is ego. Studies have shown that the primary benefit of the hand-held device is to boost the self-esteem of the owner. In the wrong hands, these devices become weapons of status. They verify that the owner is busy and important, and many users end up genuinely believing that the world will fall apart if they cannot be contacted even for a brief period. This leads to an unfortunate chain of behaviour that can include disturbing everyone else in public places, ignoring people in face-to-face conversations, blanking members of one's own family and failing to pay attention in meetings. The rap sheet is longer but the point is made. So many executives now check their emails under the table in meetings that it has become known as the BlackBerry Prayer.

The sharp end is that the worse the news, the more likely it is to come via a computer or device. That's cowardice. As we know, looking someone dead in the eye and delivering bad news is not easy. So now lily-livered management the world over have plenty of choice with regard to the medium they wish to hide behind. The all-staff email can cover a multitude of nasties without the writer ever having to face the people affected. Those who are paid well to make tough decisions should examine the manner in which they communicate with their people.

Don't assume you can handle it all at once

In days gone by, if you had a couple of letters in the post or a few phone calls then you could deal with them. But how many messages can someone deal with in a day? There is a numerical limit and an executive receiving 100 emails per hour has surely reached it. Wouldn't it be good if an email inbox would only take a maximum of, say, ten messages a day? The rest would wait in a queue until the recipient was ready for the next in line. The moral for individuals in the modern world is: don't assume you can handle it all at once. You might be able to, but if not, then it's your job to make some changes to how the communication is flowing in your life.

The power of sequence is important here. Doing one thing at a time means that it is easier to cope with large volumes. Never touch an email more than once. Read it, then action, file or bin it. In *Getting Things Done*, David Allen recommends turning your inbox upside down and working on the principle of First In, First Out (FIFO), not Last In, First Out (LIFO) as many people do. You need a system to cope with the huge volumes. Those who approach their inbox randomly will usually be swamped. A colleague used to sweep all her paperwork into the bin each night on the grounds that if it were that important, someone else would have it. Those who have had a technological meltdown and lost everything usually experience a short moment of panic followed by extreme elation and relief. There are rarely repercussions either. Most colleagues and friends don't notice. If this is true, then deleting everything every few months could be a very good strategy for coping with communication indeed.

The right medium for the right message

To communicate well with technology, we need the right medium for the right message and a clear understanding of the suitability of each for the task. Intersecting monologues won't do. Almost everything we do involves the need for effective communication and yet often we really aren't very good at it. Methods of communicating are always changing. The rank order of possible communication methods, based on the likelihood of you being correctly understood, is talking face-to-face, a telephone conversation, then an email, text or instant message. With regard to effectiveness, the first beats all the rest by a hundred to one.

Some people seem to think that once they have fired off a message they can wash their hands of something. Nothing could be further from the truth. Among the possible reasons for this are:

▶ The message never arrives.

▶ The intended recipient never reads it.

▶ They are not there.

▶ They are too busy or disorganized.

▶ They read it but they don't agree.

▶ They want to discuss it with you before doing anything.

Remember this

We have so many methods of communicating that we frequently choose the wrong one.

So as a high-quality communication method, email and other messaging methods leave much to be desired. But there are other more subtle possibilities lurking too:

▶ Most people don't check their messages before sending, so that any errors can make them look sloppy or impede what they are trying to say.

▶ Your original message or reply is often forwarded to someone you don't know.

▶ The presentation format is often in the hands of the receiver, not the sender.

▶ People you don't know about are sometimes blind copied on the original for political purposes that you know nothing about.

The sort of chaos that can ensue from these possibilities shouldn't really require any further elaboration. Suffice to say that any communication method that has these pitfalls needs to be treated with extreme caution. Some careful thought will always lead to a better result. So think before you dive in and try talking to people – it is much more charming and almost always more effective.

Case study: Escalating Email

Here's the transcript of an email trail between Paul, an Account Director at an advertising agency, and his client Vicky, the Marketing Director of a major bank. As you can see, it got out of hand unnecessarily.

From: Vicky@majorbank.com

To: Paul@adagency.co.uk

Hi Paul. Just dashing into an awayday. Can you get the team to do a competitive review of the last year? I need it for the CEO by Friday? Thanks.

From: Paul@adagency.co.uk

To: Vicky@majorbank.com

Wow. That's a big project! Very unlikely we can do such a thing in three days flat. I'll call to discuss which competitors, which media, and how much detail we need.

From: Paul@adagency.co.uk

To: Vicky@majorbank.com

Hi Vicky. I left a message earlier today but you're not picking up. Please call urgently so we can discuss the competitive review you need.

From: Vicky@majorbank.com

To: Paul@adagency.co.uk

I've been in an awayday all day as I said – now we've lost a day. Please just get the review underway. I'll be back in session tomorrow but the deadline still remains.

From: Paul@adagency.co.uk

To: Vicky@majorbank.com

Just received your email. I'm sorry but realistically we can't start on this without a proper brief. There are so many variables that we could set in train all sorts of irrelevant work and lines of enquiry. Please call – then we can work it out and get as much done as the time allows.

From: Vicky@majorbank.com

To: Paul@adagency.co.uk

I haven't got time to write a brief – just round up all the other banks we usually look at and get their media spends for the last year. Friday deadline still stands – I am seeing the CEO at 11am.

From: Paul@adagency.co.uk

To: Vicky@majorbank.com

Vicky. Sorry but I am flying blind here. Please find attached a list of competitive banks and confirm they are what you want looked at. We can get topline figures for quarters 1–4 – a summary sheet for each, with a breakdown by medium (TV, press, etc.) but with no detail on programme selection or costs. That's all we can do in time.

From: Vicky@majorbank.com

To: Paul@adagency.co.uk

The CEO insists we have programme selection too – please include.

From: Paul@adagency.co.uk

To: Vicky@majorbank.com

Can we talk? I have left more messages and we really need to discuss this. As I mentioned, we won't be able to get that level of detail in time for tomorrow morning...

From: Vicky@majorbank.com

To: Paul@adagency.co.uk

It's crucial – we have to have it...JFDI!

From: Paul@adagency.co.uk

To: Vicky@majorbank.com

I just called again to discuss. Please pick up.

As you can see, this communication isn't working and eventually it collapses completely. Email is a perfectly valid medium but it doesn't suit every conversation. Email is not an urgent medium. It should not be used to delegate without proper explanation. There's nothing particularly wrong with the original request but with little definition and a nasty deadline it should have been a phone call.

As the client hides behind two days of meetings and refuses to speak in person, the agency loses vital time and becomes increasingly exasperated. Paul tries to change the medium by calling, but Vicky won't pick up and keeps reverting to email, which will never unclog the problem.

Next time you have a communication issue, consider whether changing the medium will solve the issue faster and with less stress for both sides.

How to write concisely and clearly

If you can't talk, then you are going to have to write. This is something of a dying art, so you need to put a decent argument together and get it down before you start using any form of technology to convey it. Don't just start writing. Draw up a shape and prepare a draft first. This could apply to a detailed email response, a document or even a letter. Interestingly, these days it is something of a novelty to receive a letter. So much the better if it is – shock, horror! – hand-written. The effect is so much more powerful.

Try following these steps.

Work out what you are trying to achieve
Start by asking whether you need to write this down at all. Should this actually be a phone call or a meeting instead? What do you want to happen when someone reads this? Write down the objectives of the exercise, and, against each one, write the desired action of the reader.

Research your intended audience
Who is going to read this? Who might read it that you haven't been told about? Are the readers similar in style and experience? What do they have in common? Are there unifying factors you can draw on which will make the readers more likely to agree? What attention span do they have? What frame of reference will best allow you to make your points? Are the readers potentially willing, reluctant or hostile? If they are hostile, what might persuade them?

Research your subject

Do you really know what you are writing about? Could you know a bit more? If so, go looking for information. Are there sources that might help? Use positive arguments. Disproving the opposite case does not make yours. Using negative arguments makes you sound negative. Amass killer facts. They should be true, from a reliable source and fundamental to your case. If you make assertions, consider whether you would believe them if you were the reader, particularly if they tend to the sceptical. If you are dubious, find the evidence to support your points or change the phrasing to make them more opinion based.

Choose an accurate and engaging title

If you are starting a debate, write a provocative question. If you are trying to persuade the reader of a particular stance, state it. If your purpose is information, keep it factual and free of loaded words. If you want to generate emotion, put it in before the subject matter. Play around with the chosen title and constantly check it against the relevance of the content as it develops. There is nothing wrong with changing the title once you have written the content, as long as it is an improvement.

Create a decent structure

The better the plan, the better the writing. Try writing the complete argument in no more than a dozen points on one page. It needs an introduction, a beginning, a middle and an end. The introduction explains what this is for. The beginning opens the case with relevant information. It should include a 'grabber' – something which makes the reader pay attention. This could be a quote, a fact, a comparison, something they don't know or a controversial statement. This is followed by your main themes – preferably no more than three. The main themes may need supporting material or evidence. This is fine, but consider whether it interrupts the argument or is essential. If it gets in the way, put it in an appendix or an attachment. The end needs to reprise the main themes, have a strong recommendation and make it clear what you want the reader to do.

Now add a bit of colour

Always ask yourself: have I heard this before? If you have, think of something more original. Imagine you are having a conversation with someone. How would you phrase it to them out loud? Don't make the language flowery. Add colour with relevant, distinctive words. When you have written something, read it out loud. If it sounds ludicrous, change it. Keep it simple and don't get weird, unless you are providing a counterpoint to the simplicity of your own proposal or want to shock to make a point. Review the whole thing for colour, pace, rhythm and emotion.

Avoid cliché and bullshit

As with the talking advice in the last chapter, imagine you were reading it to your mum or a mate in the pub. Do you feel stupid? If yes, change it. Would they understand it? If no, change it. Use the spotting waffle guide to check for false arguments, circular arguments, repetition, incorrect conclusions (synapse jumps), spurious sources, irrelevance and weak points. Most cases add weak points at the end that undermine the strong, valid points at the beginning. It is better to have two or three strong ones than a shopping list of increasingly weak ones.

Edit several times

Shorter is always better. Be relevant, rational and ruthless. Remember the difference between a conclusion and a summary. A conclusion is when you have argued a point and concluded. You can do this on several different points to build your case. When you have made them all, the summary draws together everything you have said. It therefore repeats the conclusions and repeats any recommendations. It is essential that the summary does not make any new points at all. If it does, your structure is wrong.

Dealing with writer's block

Most people talk faster and more fluently than they write and can hear themselves a few sentences ahead of the writing on the page. So when you do not know what to write, try saying out loud what you want to say. Then write it down. In extreme cases, record yourself and listen back to it. Remember, writer's block is temporary. If nothing is happening, break the pattern by doing something physical or different. If that doesn't work, do the most boring thing in your in-tray and come back to it later.

Check with someone else

Give it the overnight test if you can. You will always spot something in the morning that you didn't the day before and you will probably have had another idea. This is your own quality control test. Edit it ruthlessly, then show it to someone else. If they don't understand your main points, express them differently. Even when you are happy with the whole thing, get someone else to proofread it. Your eye may read misspelled words as correct because you wrote them yourself.

Once you have done all of this you are ready to transmit via whichever technology you have decided is the most appropriate.

Technology morals

Communication is complex, so don't just dive in to the nearest technology and start transmitting. Think hard about how you want your life to be affected by it. Make it work for you. Tame it. Don't be a slave to it. You may feel that you have no say in how you interact with your technology, but that's not true. The way it currently is doesn't have to be the way it's going to be. A full review of your approach can reap great dividends. There are many morals to be learned from the way in which much modern technology is used. Here are the most important.

Think hard about how you want it to affect your life
Don't just accept that everyone else is doing it, so you have to too. Pause to decide what technology you would like to have as part of your armoury.

Make it work for you, not the other way round
You don't have to use any technology you don't want to. Consider your ideal set-up and reorganize things to match that if possible.

Only turn it on for specific times each day
Map out a regime and stick to it. You will liberate free time to do lots of other interesting things.

Turn it off when you need to get things done
Constant distraction simply leads to frustration and half-baked ideas and projects.

Don't assume you can handle it all at once
You probably can't, so be honest with yourself and make changes.

Don't hide behind it
Doing so suppresses your true nature and is usually unpleasant for everyone else.

Don't let it lure you into doing inappropriate things
Illegal activities are clearly out, but also beware drunk and angry communication – no one wins.

Do not let it come between you and those you care about
If you spend more time with a machine than your partner or family, then something is wrong.

Do not confuse what it can do with tasks that require humanity
Always go for the human option before you use a machine to do the job.

Do not assume that any job is done by the technology alone
It's not done until someone has done it. That's either you or the person you have asked, but bear in mind that they might not even agree, let alone do what you ask.

Unlock the facts
'The email of the species is deadlier than the mail.'

A new communication etiquette

Many people just dive in to the nearest technology when they need to convey something. This is not always advisable. It pays to pause briefly and consider the best method. Always start at the human end of the spectrum and leave machines and technology till last. You should aim to meet, call, write and in that order. If you can't meet, then call. If you can't call, then write carefully. Here are some resolutions for each stage.

MEET
When you secure a meeting, get organized straightaway
If you leave it to the last minute you won't communicate as well as you want to.

Research everything thoroughly
People who don't know their stuff get rumbled quickly and are less persuasive.

Give them a list of ways to fix things
Alternatives provide lots to talk about and plenty of ways forward.

Include things that you could do, even if you have never done them
That's how you get to do new things.

Ask what is on their mind at the moment
Let people identify their own needs.

Listen more than you talk
Otherwise you won't learn anything.

Be more positive than everyone else in every meeting
Who wants to have a meeting with a boring, negative person?

Never be late
It's rude and suggests that you don't care.

Be spontaneous and act naturally
Pretending to be someone you're not never works.

CALL

Prepare what you are going to say
What about x? Or y? Very well, what about z?

Don't use jargon
If you waffle, they won't get it.

Tell it like it is
Don't sugar-coat things. If it's bad, be honest.

Offer to solve their issue quickly
No one wants to wait if they need something.

Be natural and human
Don't go into business mode. Be your normal self.

Don't call it 'cold calling'
You might think it's cold, but the other person might not.

WRITE

We have already covered a lot about how to write appropriately, but in summary:

▶ Only write if you cannot meet or call.

▶ Write concisely and clearly.

▶ Check it before you send it.

▶ If it's complicated or emotional, pause before sending.

Unlock the facts

Work out what you want to achieve and then decide if it requires a piece of technology.

Communication can be very complicated, so don't just dive in with any old words and any random technology. Think hard about what you want to say and how best to say it. Choose the most appropriate medium for the task and pause to check everything before you send it. This will make everything you generate more thoughtful and help you to communicate better all round.

Taming Technology Tips for Communicating

1 **Make human interaction your first port of call every time**
Always ask yourself: which is better for this job, a person or a machine? If it's the latter, then try to get some humanity into the process. Add some character and make it clearly recognizable as your style. If at all possible, don't use technology to do the job.

2 **Don't hide behind technology**
If it's tough and nasty, don't be a coward. People can take tough news, particularly if it is delivered with integrity and a little care. Do not use technology as a shield to avoid the issue. In particular, consider how you would feel if you were receiving this news or information via technology. Put yourself in the shoes of the recipient. Now choose the most sympathetic medium for the task.

3 **Don't assume you can handle it all at once**
You might be able to, but you might not. Those who claim they can are often the ones who can't. People who say they are good at multitasking are usually the ones who aren't. There's no disgrace in saying enough is enough. In fact, it may even be a good thing to do. Recognize when the time has come for changes and then make some.

4 **Choose the right medium for the message**

Think carefully about the point of what you wish to communicate. Would this be better as a chat in person? Or a phone call? Is this email, text, tweet or instant message really necessary? Does this need to be said at all? Take the extra moment to think about it. Choosing the right medium can help enormously and sometimes you might conclude that something is best not said at all.

5 **Practise concise and clear writing**

Once you have decided that it needs to be written down, think carefully about the shape of it. Plan and draft before launching into something that isn't well thought through. Writing something out can be an important step towards clarity, even if the written word isn't your final chosen method.

6 **Review your technology and make some changes**

Cast your eye over all your technology. Is it what you want? Does it work for you? Does it allow you to communicate effectively? A lot of devices seemed good a while ago but are no longer relevant or helpful. Assess what you have and see if you are happy with the mix of your technology. If not, make changes that fall more in your favour.

7 **Consider the new communication etiquette**

Meet if you can. Call if you can't meet. Write if you can't call, but think carefully about the content and method. In any event, try to increase the proportion of interactions that are personal rather than remote.

8 **Develop ways to cope with techno rage**

If technology drives you nuts from time to time, try to identify why and what the main culprits are. Then invent ways to reduce stress by using that technology less, under less time pressure or by understanding better how it works.

9 **If an email, text or instant message conversation is getting out of hand, stop**

Conversations that escalate into ping-pong slanging matches are unhealthy. Recognize as soon as possible when this is on the verge of happening. Resist the temptation to get involved in tit-for-tat exchanges. Break the pattern by picking up the phone or turning up in person.

10   **Don't dash to the nearest technology as a matter of course**
Don't make technology a default option. Work out what you wish
to do first or what you think. Then decide how best to communicate
that to someone else. Don't start firing off instructions or messages
until you know why.

Focus points

✱ Human interaction will never die out completely, but technology
is doing a pretty good job of getting in the way. Always make
communicating in person your first port of call. Only use technology
where you really need to.

✱ Don't assume you can handle it all at once – the chances are you
can't. Modern levels of inbound material are so huge that the average
person can't cope.

✱ Review the sheer volume of your interactions and try to come up with
a better approach based on some of the suggestions in this chapter.

✱ Choosing the right medium for the right message is important. No
one medium is intrinsically bad, but most have significant deficiencies,
particularly with sensitive subject matter. The touchier the issue, the
less appropriate technology is likely to be.

✱ A new communication etiquette is needed, especially for those who
have experienced nothing other than the current technological age.
Not everything has to be texted or emailed. Take the trouble to think
about your whole approach to communicating with others.

✱ Try some of the Taming Technology Tips for Communicating. Start with
one or two. If they work, keep going. If they don't, try some others.

Next step
**Chapter 6 puts things into action, with or without
your chosen technology.**

Doing

In this chapter you will learn:

▶ *If our activities are making us happy. It is only by getting stuff done that we feel any sense of purpose and satisfaction.*

▶ *The two types of tasks: quantitative and qualitative. Try and balance both types throughout your day.*

▶ *Not to aim for perfection. Good enough will do and means we can get more done.*

▶ *That activity doesn't mean action. You can be very busy but not actually achieve anything. 'Rapid sequential tasking' is far more efficient than multitasking.*

▶ *To consider an 'anti list'. What AREN'T you going to do? Take on less and DO MORE.*

Human beings and human doings

We are human beings, but just being isn't enough for us. We need to be human doings. It is only by getting stuff done that we feel any sense of purpose and satisfaction. Every day we can choose from hundreds of activities, so the question is whether we are doing the right blend of things to make us happy. In relation to our technology, the answer will often be no. If we do too much of the wrong stuff, then that often means we do not have enough time left for the right stuff. We need to be able to distinguish between which parts of our relationship with our machines matter and which don't so we can make better use of our time.

There are two main types of task – quantitative and qualitative. If it's quantitative, the job just needs doing, full stop. You can tick the jobs off numerically and view them as a quantity of things to be done. If it's qualitative, the job needs doing well. The quality can be demonstrably better than if it is done badly, and excellence should be your goal. There is a massive difference between the two. It is crucial to take the time to distinguish between the two when you are sitting at a computer or about to make a phone call. If it is quantitative, then it should be fast and functional. If qualitative, take your time, plan carefully and do it properly. These principles apply to any medium and are particularly important if you are jumping between tasks and different technology (but try not to do this). Plan your tasks and spend an appropriate amount of time using one method. Then pause, take a break and move on to the next.

Unlock the facts

Quantitative tasks can neither be done well nor badly – they just need doing. Qualitative tasks need proper time and attention.

So what does *not* work is if you simply sit in front of your computer or pick up your device and start typing. There will be no shape to your efforts. Instead, take any of your lists and separate the tasks by those that simply need doing and those that need to be done well. It is hard to generalize about this because it depends somewhat on your job and lifestyle but the percentage of functional tasks you typically have to do is likely to be high. Everything of this nature should be done as fast and clinically as possible and with no delay. Many people like to do these tasks first, so as to allow proper thinking time for the quality jobs.

Should you choose not to take this approach, then it is highly likely that you will have a barcode day. This is a concept introduced by Matt Kingdon in a book called *Sticky Wisdom*. Picture a barcode. It is made up of many tiny slivers. Now imagine that this is a snapshot of your working day or any unit of time, even an hour at your desk. If you blindly sit at a computer or device and try to cover as many tasks as possible, but in no particular order, you will be barcoding, or, put passively, you will be barcoded by technology. In other words, bittiness and interruptions will force you to work in smaller and smaller chunks to the detriment of any proper attention on one important thing. Don't let technology do this to you.

Confronting the devil

I once had a conversation with the owner of a company that had grown over ten years to have around 600 staff. He was concerned that the original feel of a start-up had been lost underneath too much process and administration. It felt like the company was slowing down, and the suspicion was that too many people were doing a lot of things that they didn't need to do. Although the message from the top had always been to be smart and get on with it, the feeling was that this attitude was on the wane. The way he expressed it was that people 'needed convincing that the devil is there'.

This is a crucial breakthrough moment in being able to do things effectively with technology, because many edicted people do not believe that there is a problem in the first place. Let's acknowledge that there must be some people who are so well organized and have such a well-balanced relationship with their technology that they can handle everything that's thrown at them every day with comfort. For all the rest of us, we need to tame it. When it comes to doing, we need to take three steps.

1 Admit that the devil is there.

2 Confront the issue.

3 Adopt a new attitude and approach.

So, step one is confession time. 'My name is Kevin Duncan and I'm a technoholic. I admit that on certain days, in fact more often than I would like, I cannot get everything done that I would like because I keep getting interrupted by one form of technology or another. Sometimes, it's the phone, sometimes it's email, and other times I just get distracted pottering about on social media.' Try this exercise yourself.

Step two is confronting the technology devil. An endless bombardment of inbound material simply cannot be endured forever by one individual. Someone is going to crack, and it is more likely to be a human than a machine. And something important is going to slip through the net. The machismo language of the online world doesn't help. We are apparently supposed to be 'always on', available 24/7/365, or, according to one device manufacturer, capable of doing the impossible every day. It's unsustainable and unrealistic. Those who have a balanced view are able to see it for what it is and laugh at it by calling edicted people Crackberries because they have an addictive immediate response to every incoming message.

Unlock the facts

Sitting in front of a computer or device and simply starting to type doesn't work.

Step three is adopting a new attitude and approach, and that means setting up a new system. Your ability to get things done, whether involving a machine or otherwise, will improve dramatically if you make some simple changes. Start by setting aside thinking time. Use a system or draw up an organized list for tasks. Separate them by quantitative or qualitative. Divide them by those that require technology and those that don't.

Map out your time to reflect the balance. Then, either do all the non-technology tasks before going near a machine or do all the technological tasks first and then walk away from your computer or device to do the rest. This will lead to a more productive result in both online and ordinary activities, will prevent you from having a barcode day and will liberate better quality time for the jobs that warrant it.

Progress not perfection

Is your very best perfect? I doubt it. Mine never is. This is the dilemma with striving for perfection. There is nothing wrong with it as a life philosophy but it simply cannot be applied to everything that needs to be done. The more frenetic we are, the more we have to make do with 'good enough will do' and get on with it. Never was this approach more appropriate than online. The debate rages on two levels. The first (high level) theme is that a huge amount of unedited stuff appears on the internet. Fans say this is great because it generates a superb melting pot in which ideas can be exchanged and co-created. Detractors dismiss it as the random rantings of amateurs who are not subject to any editing. At the second (micro) level billions of messages are exchanged every day that contain typographical and grammatical errors. Objectors feel this is a case of standards slipping and fans say so what? We are communicating, so let us get on with it and stay away if you don't want to join in.

As with so many things in life, perhaps somewhere in the middle is the place to be. If your online reputation is important, then make sure that the quality of what you produce is of a standard that befits what you are trying to achieve. Tasks can be undone by poor execution, so there is a link between quality and successfully getting things done. On the other hand, this can be pushed too far. Striving for high quality is great, but being a perfectionist can be a tremendous burden, particularly when the technology is there to make your life easier, not make it all more complicated. There are two fundamental problems with perfection:

1 Perfection may not exist.

2 Perfection may never quite arrive.

Unlock the facts

Don't wait for perfection – run with what you've got and fix it as you go.

When it comes to technology, how can anyone ever prove that something is perfect? Perfection is a qualitative notion and is therefore unhelpful for the purposes of getting things done. People often fall into the trap of making an ill-judged connection between success and perfection. And yet nothing could be more imperfect than those people and projects that eventually achieve success. Their road to achievement is usually littered with false starts and mishaps. Successful products are preceded by many prototypes, many of them defective. The more mistakes you make, the more you learn, and this is especially true of working with technology. It is changing all the time, and there is always so much more to discover, so it is crucial that you make mistakes in order to make progress. Striving to do something better is admirable, but do bear in mind that perfection may be a mythical construct that can never be achieved. As the old saying goes, if you want to succeed, double your failure rate. Or, in the words of Paul Arden, author of *Whatever You Think, Think The Opposite*: 'Instead of waiting for perfection, run with what you've got, and fix it as you go.'

Action not activity

If you like a mantra to help you do things more effectively, try these:

▶ Efficiency is a sophisticated form of laziness.

▶ Don't confuse movement with progress.

▶ Take on less, do more.

▶ Action not activity.

▶ Outcome not output.

Efficiency is a sophisticated form of laziness means that the better organized you are, the easier it is to generate free time. You can then use that time for whatever you want. People who are constantly in essay crisis mode lack control and do not usually achieve what they want. So when it comes to your technology, plan more and flap less. Random events and creative thoughts are great but you will have more of them if you create the right conditions.

Don't confuse movement with progress means don't get distracted by lots of movement that generates no forward motion. All talk and no action gets you nowhere. How many times have you observed in life that a lot appears to be happening, but in fact, nothing much really is? This is what the Italians call the English disease: rushing around creating the impression that things are happening but with no real tangible results. You can sit at a computer all day and not really get anywhere, although your boss might think you are working hard. Do not generate a smokescreen of activity to disguise the fact that important things are not being done.

Take on less, do more means paying careful attention to the nature and scope of what you are doing at any given time. Technology can be deceptive. It can hide a mountain of tasks because there is no visible untidy desk. Who knows how many new tasks have arrived in your email inbox at the same time as your acceptance of a busy new project? Screen all your machines for new work before accepting more and consider saying no politely.

Action not activity means getting to the decisive point of action rather than diving into a blizzard of activity. They are not the same thing. What's so clever about being busy? Any fool can appear to be permanently busy, or truly be busy, particularly if they hide behind technology. If you want something to happen, concentrate on the action, not on activity that makes it look as though action is occurring.

Outcome not output is a different way of expressing the same thing. A lot of output makes it look as though much is happening, when frequently it isn't. If you achieve something excellent, who cares how you got there? If you have a great idea, who cares whether it happened in a flash, or over two weeks or several years? Generating huge amounts of stuff (output) may have nothing to do with the end result (outcome). So before you spend days at a computer producing endless documents and spreadsheets, or firing off email after email, work out your desired outcome and work backwards from there.

Case study: Multitasking Monica and Perfectionist Pam

Now here's a story about efficiency at work – a sort of modern time and motion study. Monica and Pam worked at a charity. The company was permanently understaffed, with far too much to do and not enough people to do it all. Both of them got through a lot, but in very different ways.

Monica was the kind of person who prided herself on being a consummate multitasker. She always had stacks on the go at once and liked to tell everyone how busy she was. All the cues round her desk proved the point – huge towers of files, boxes of archiving material, numerous panels open on her computer at any given time, several phones always going off, meetings wall-to-wall and a general impression of lots and lots going on. No observer could conclude anything other than that she was clearly very busy and working hard at it.

But there was a flaw in the plan – she wasn't really getting much done. All the activity was effectively a smokescreen for the fact things were rarely completed. Hundreds of tasks were started, and very much labelled as being 'work in progress', but nothing was actually finished. So that meant lots of things underway, tantalizing everyone else into thinking they might arrive soon, when in fact they were just part of a messy and rather disorganized queue of work that often didn't arrive anywhere.

Pam was quite different. She was a self-confessed perfectionist. Everything had to be 'just so'. This had a number of unfortunate consequences. First, everything Pam got involved with took ages. She always insisted on making further tweaks, regardless of whether anyone else had asked for changes. This meant her work was either late or right up against the deadline. Second, it made for slow progress. If her work had gone out on the second draft instead of the sixth, she could have handled twice as much work, and the quality would have been indistinguishable to most colleagues and customers. Third, and perhaps importantly, being a perfectionist drove her nuts, because she never thought anything was quite good enough. This led to under-confidence and low self-esteem.

It took any boss or colleague looking at these two going about their daily work a while to work out the (unintentional) deception. Both Monica and Pam were diligent, conscientious and well intentioned. To start with, the impression they generated was positive – keen, active and committed to the cause. But after a month or so the flaws would emerge. In Monica's case, this was a 'flatter to deceive' deception – it looked like lots was going on, and in a way it was, but in truth nothing particularly helpful was being done. In Pam's case, the rigour was laudable, but the output was painfully slow and the angst that went with every project was palpable.

And the moral of the story? There are two. The first is that those who claim to be great at multitasking rarely are. They usually have a lot started but not necessarily finished. It is better to start and finish something before moving on to the next thing. The second is that perfection doesn't exist. It is good to work to high standards, but constantly tinkering takes forever, erodes margin and drives the perfectionist mad.

Multitasking and rapid sequential tasking

A couple of years ago I had just put the bread in the toaster when my partner asked me a question about holiday plans. *'I'll think about that in a minute,'* I replied, *'I'm just making toast.'* I wasn't joking. It's classic male stuff – we can only do one thing at once apparently. The debate rages on to the point of cliché – women can multitask and men can't. As a male myself I am happy to concede the point: I am not good at doing several things at the same time and technology has now made this problem a whole lot worse. When confronted by many panels on a computer, I am like a mosquito in a nudist camp. I know what I want to do but I don't know where to start. So what can men do if this is truly the case? How can they be any good at getting lots of stuff done all at once?

Unlock the facts

The idea of being 'always on' is unsustainable.

The secret lies in rapid sequential tasking. Just because men can't do lots at the same time does not mean that they can't do lots in a sequence, and fast. Tackling the problem of the *'Don't talk to me, I'm making toast'* syndrome involves doing things fast, but one after the other. If you have ten emails to send, do them one at a time in one half-hour session then close the email function. If you have three presentations to write, have a PowerPoint session then close the software. If you need to do some accounting work, spend an hour on spreadsheets and then close it down. If you need to make six phone calls, then move away from your desk and do those one at a time. Changing media like this is good for variety and may even force you to take a short break in-between each blast.

This sequential approach is far more effective than having everything on the go at once. It also has one distinct advantage over multitasking. As we saw in Chapter 1, studies show that the most persistent multitaskers perform badly in a variety of tasks. They don't focus as well, they are more easily distractible and they are weaker at shifting from one thing to another. In fact, they are worse at it than people who do not usually multitask. There is a strong suspicion that in the case of much multitasking, all the tasks may well have been started, but they may not have been finished. This is a crucial point. Although the beginning of any task is clearly vital, it isn't over until it's over. The beauty of rapid sequential tasking is that you don't move on to the next task until you have finished the last one, making it much easier to cope with whatever technology throws at you next.

Anti lists

An anti list is a list of what you are *not* going to do. This is a crucial aid to taming technology and establishing what you *are* going to do. There are various ways in which writing this list can really help. It establishes:

▶ What you will never do with your technology.

▶ What you don't want to do with your technology.

► What you won't do today with your technology.

► What action really will help achieve the task (with or without technology).

All are tremendously helpful to know and could be equally valid depending on the nature of the job. Firstly, it is crucial to know what you will never do with your technology. Whatever these things are, they are vital components of your standards, principles, personal character and, vitally, your relationship with your machines. If you have never done the exercise before, take a sheet of paper (or tap into your laptop or device) 'I will never…' and fill in the rest of the sentence. There may be several pledges. It's a very therapeutic process.

Secondly, you will clarify what you do and don't want to do. We all have to do things that we don't really want to and obviously some are much worse than others. Identifying what you don't *want* to do with your technology versus what you will *never* do is a very helpful comparison.

Remember this
We do far too much of the wrong stuff, which often means we do not have enough time left for the right stuff.

The third point, what you won't do with your technology today, is a temporal one and one of priority. Prevaricators who make a life's work out of putting everything off require significant help here. Tasks do not improve in quality if they are delayed. The value of establishing what you won't do today is so that you can do more important things first, not so that you never do them. Also, today is just one unit of time to describe when the task will be done. It could equally apply to the next five minutes, the next hour, this morning, tomorrow, this week, this month or this year. Don't become a victim of time. You must be acutely aware that the longer the unit of time, the less likely it is that the task will be done.

Finally, consider what action really will help to achieve a task. It may not require any technology at all. Draw up some principles and attitudes to your machines and try hard to stick to them. Be stubborn. Do less and get more done.

When doing nothing is best

As far as we can tell, it is generally better to do something rather than nothing. Presumably that's because action gives us a sense of purpose and inaction suggests idleness. But here's a contrary view – sometimes doing nothing is the smartest move. This is a view held by Ofer Azer, a lecturer at the School of Management at Ben-Gurion University of the Negev in Israel. He argues that when people are under pressure the urge to take action is powerful. Goalkeepers who let in penalties feel better if they have at least moved. Traders losing money on shares feel better if they sell, even if they make a loss. And politicians are always tempted to 'do something' when the economy is doing poorly. When it comes to technology, we should certainly choose the 'do nothing' route more often.

One man who has an interesting take on this whole area is Ricardo Semler, a Brazilian who runs a massive set of companies and insists on working in an unconventional way. He likes to question everything and in his book *The Seven-Day Weekend* he asks, among other things:

▷ Why are we able to answer emails on Sundays, but unable to go to the movies on Monday afternoons?

▷ Why do we think the opposite of work is leisure, when in fact it is idleness?

There are two levels here. One is that doing nothing can be a vital part of work, and vice versa, as we saw with the bleisure time phenomenon in Chapter 1. Even when you have a vast amount to do, it pays to pause and reflect. If work can intrude on your leisure time, then leisure should be allowed to play a part in your work. If introduced appropriately, it should improve your relationship with your technology.

The second level is the balance between work and idleness. Tom Hodgkinson edits a magazine called *The Idler*, so he should know all about it. As far as he is concerned, society today extols the virtues of efficiency and frowns upon laziness, but as Oscar Wilde once said, 'doing nothing is hard work.' As modern life grows ever more demanding, we may well feel the odds stacking against us, so we need an antidote to the work-obsessed culture that puts so many obstacles between us and our dreams.

There are benefits to doing nothing. For example, lying in bed half awake – what sleep researchers call the hypnagogic dream state – is positively beneficial to health and happiness and can help prepare you mentally for the problems and tasks ahead. It is also the time when some of our best ideas come to us. The rational 'overmind' largely ignores the emotional or spiritual 'undermind', but this is where we build up strength to cope with life's struggles. Nobody knows why but sleep can solve many of our problems. Apparently insurmountable problems almost always look better in the morning. As John Steinbeck said: 'It is a common experience that a problem difficult at night is resolved in the morning after the committee of sleep has worked on it.'

Doing nothing is always worth considering as a first option. We often feel (or are made to feel?) guilty about taking time off and we shouldn't. Americans now work an extra month a year compared with 30 years ago, averaging nine hours a day. Life is supposed to be getting easier, but we still elect to overwork. As such, those overdoing it in the workplace would do well to take a little time out, if only to check whether they lack balance between work and relaxation. Doing nothing with your machines must surely be worth consideration, if only for a short while each day or week just to change the pattern.

Confront the doing part of your life in the context of technology. Distinguish between how you are going to get things done and the most appropriate method for doing it. Work out what you are *not* going to do and make best use of your time to do the most important things.

Taming Technology Tips for Doing

1 Admit that the devil is there and confront it

You may be perfectly happy with the way you do things with technology. But if it is all a bit overwhelming, it might be worth admitting there is an issue and confronting it. Try keeping a note of how long you spend per day or week using technology. You might surprise yourself at the amount. If the balance is wrong, then make some changes.

2 Adopt a new approach to doing things with technology

Change the pattern. Plan your approach first. Group together tasks that require the same technology. Estimate how long it will take and try to set time limits. Move smoothly from one group of jobs to another and take breaks in-between. Being disciplined about how much time you spend on certain tasks will increase your effectiveness when doing them and increase variety.

3 Distinguish between quantitative and qualitative tasks

Quantitative tasks can be done neither well nor badly – they just need to be done. Get these out of the way first and fast so that you can free up time to concentrate on the important, qualitative tasks, whether you are using technology or not. Most people like a balance of both types of task, so try not to let this become skewed. The occasional day just doing functional (quantitative) tasks may be therapeutic, but a mixture is usually best.

4 Go for progress, not perfection

Don't spend hours at a computer making something absolutely perfect. Do your best of course, but remember that perfection is a matter of opinion. Someone else may well have a different view and ask for changes anyway, so give it your best shot and fix it as you go along. You'll get more done and be less stressed. Also, ask yourself frequently whether the task in hand does indeed require technology – if you conclude that it doesn't, then there's no point in spending hours at a computer perfecting it anyway.

5 Concentrate on action, not activity

Just because a lot is going on doesn't necessarily mean you are getting anywhere. Always ask yourself *why* you are using a certain machine and *what* you are trying to achieve. One precise action could be more effective than a day's worth of frenetic activity. Create time to reflect on this as often as you can.

6 **If you can't do multitasking, try rapid sequential tasking**
   If you can do it all at once then go for it. If not, then don't try. Take one thing at a time and don't start anything else until you have finished it. Then move on to the next. The overall effect should be that you get more done and feel more fulfilled.

7 **Try writing an anti list**
   Lists are great, but if there is too much on them, they can be daunting. Try writing a list of what you are *not* going to do. It is not a waste of time. It tells you a lot about your priorities with technology and is great for morale. Use the list to eliminate fruitless tasks on your task list.

8 **Take on less and do more**
   When a machine asks or tells you to do something, consider saying no, politely of course. People who take on too much usually let someone down, and that someone may well be you. By taking on less, you will get more done of the things that really matter to you. Use your experience to head off requests with better ideas to address whatever the issues are.

9 **Consider doing nothing**
   Every now and again, take no action whatsoever. How many times has an issue been resolved after a trail of ten emails before you even answered the first one? Let things go hang sometimes and try to do nothing with your machines for a certain period every day and every week.

10 **Think about doing and being**
    Pause occasionally and consider the link between what you do and who you are. Actions say a lot about you, and with so many of these arriving via various forms of technology, they can quickly become your outward persona. Do you define who you are or does your technology?

Focus points

✳ Concentrate on progress not perfection. Keep standards high of course, but don't slave at something until you've flogged it to death. Consider revealing work in progress to see if others agree with your general direction – then polish it up if they concur.

✳ Put your effort into action, not activity. Activity fills time and may get you nowhere. Specific action gets things done. There is a difference.

✳ Multitasking and rapid sequential tasking are not the same thing. Many multitaskers have lots of things started, but none of them finished. Do not have too much underway at once. Only move on to the next thing when you have finished the last thing – that's rapid sequential tasking.

✳ Sometimes, doing nothing is the best option. We don't always have to sprint into action. If something is complicated, take the time to think. You may conclude that nothing needs to be done – at least for the moment.

✳ Try some of the Taming Technology Tips for Doing. Start with one or two. If they work, keep going. If they don't, try some others.

Next step
Chapter 7 draws it all together so that you can decide on your personal style and determine your overall attitude to technology.

Being

In this chapter you will learn:

▶ *We can all be better. We should define our own characters and not allow them to be defined by our possessions or technology.*

▶ *Humility + honesty + humour = happiness. Being well adjusted helps you to cope with extremes, to laugh at mishaps and to shrug off adverse conditions.*

▶ *To keep lots of variety in what you do to stay fresh, change things if you don't find them interesting and take regular breaks and a sensible amount of time off.*

▶ *Smaller chunks of technology mean greater clarity. Break big things down into smaller, easier to manage chunks.*

▶ *'A man is a success if he gets up in the morning and gets to bed at night, and in between he does what he wants to' Bob Dylan.*

Defined by your character or your technology?

We have looked at thinking, talking, communicating and doing, and seen that a balance is needed between engaging in any of these activities with or without our machines. And so we come full circle to the very essence of our existence – being. As Anton Chekhov pointed out, 'Any idiot can face a crisis. It is day-to-day living that wears you out.' So if you are completely obsessed with technology and could not live a day without it, we come to the nub of it all: what defines you? If the answer is you, then you have it right. If the answer is any kind of technology, then some kind of reassessment may well be needed.

Specialists who make their living from technology as experts may well be exempt from this assertion. Software developers, social media gurus and other digital natives will of course be working with machines all day. They are, however, entitled to a life outside that work and may find it therapeutic to have hobbies and outside interests that have nothing to do with technology. But for most of us, technology is an enabler that helps enormously if we use it judiciously and a monster if we let it rule our lives. When it comes to being, we can all be better. We should define our own characters, not allow them to be defined by our possessions or technology. Having a better life starts with knowing what you are all about and emanating that style.

Unlock the facts

'Any idiot can face a crisis. It's day-to-day living that wears you out.'

Ask yourself what you are like, what you are good at and what you wish to stand for. There are simple exercises that you can do to define your character. Ask yourself:

▶ If someone met you for the first time, how would they describe you?

▶ How would you describe yourself to someone you have never met?

- Are there differences between your work and outside personality?

- Is your inner self significantly different from your outward persona?

- Does your relationship with your technology affect your approach to life?

You can define your own style by asking yourself:

- Who or what is your favourite person or team?

- What qualities make them so good?

- How can those qualities inspire your approach to technology?

The stronger your sense of self-determination, the less likely you are to be dictated to by your machinery.

In pursuit of eudaemonia

Eudaemonia is an unusual word but it's a simple enough idea: the happiness resulting from a rational active life – a concept first introduced by Aristotle. It's a life-affirming idea that deserves attention and discussion in our pursuit of a manifesto for a better life. Aristotle asserted that the value of moral action lies in its capacity to provide happiness. In other words, what we do defines who we are. Here the link between doing and being is completed – the way we behave has the capacity to dictate our happiness or lack of it. So if we think carefully and then communicate and act appropriately we will be determining our quality of life directly.

A eudaemon was believed to be a benevolent, in-dwelling spirit – your soul, if you like. Eudaemonics is therefore the art or theory of happiness. Technology may or may not have any role to play in this. It is up to the individual to determine whether it could or should. One thing is certain though: technology cannot be the *only* thing that determines a person. The key lies in getting your attitude right so that you emanate a strong view. The machines can fall in line with that, not the other way round.

Aristotle also believed that it is the mark of an educated mind to be able to entertain a thought without accepting it. In the spirit of that, it is not necessary for you to agree with everything in this book, but if you grab a resolution or two and improve your relationship with your technology even a little bit, then the exercise will have been worth it.

Getting your attitude right

There are lots of things a person can do to get their attitude right and put some character into the way they operate. How you conduct yourself is crucial to the degree to which you can tame technology and get your life back. Consider these attitudinal resolutions.

You determine your own culture
You're the boss. Review your relationship with your machines. Ring some changes. Tell colleagues, bosses and family that you are taking back control. Decide on a new regime that suits your style more and makes you feel better about yourself.

As far as possible, only do things that you like
A pipe dream? Not necessarily. The apocryphal wise advice from an older lady to her daughter was to find something you love doing and find someone to pay you to do it. The more you like what you do, the less it feels like work. Design a blend of technology that gives you the same sensation.

When it comes to machines, do not distinguish between nice and nasty things to do
Sometimes stuff just has to be done, so don't waste time agonizing over how dreary you feel it is going to be. Instead, look at your machines and work out how they can take more of the burden. That's what they are there for. Consider all the tasks that you find tiresome and work out how technology can help. You might be surprised at how liberating this can be.

Remind yourself of all the positive things that technology can do
Viewed another way, try not to regard your machines with disdain. If you really hate any of them, then by all means get rid of them. But also imagine life without them and consider the alternative. This process could yield two sets of responses: confirming that you *can* do without something and confirming that you *can't*. Both are valuable discoveries.

Never use a piece of technology unless you know why you are using it
This sounds obvious and yet it may not be. Much of what we do is habitual or irrational. Why do I always have that cup of tea or coffee at that time? And why in that format? Why do I smoke? Or drink? Or check email repeatedly? Or eye my phone for messages all the time? A lot of these actions are less conscious than we think. By questioning every technological encounter, we can understand our relationship with our machines better and do something about it.

Unlock the facts

Never use a piece of technology unless you know why you are using it.

Case study: Eager-to-please Emma

Emma was a really bright student who went to a decent university and took a degree in anthropology. The subject matter was complicated and over a few years she got used to being challenged with a task, using her initiative to research it thoroughly, drawing on a wide range of material (much of it contradictory) and drawing together a well-balanced and cogent argument weighing up all the pros and cons. Whether it was a weekly essay or a full-blown dissertation, she knew how to compose an argument.

With a first-class degree she was able to get a job as a management trainee at a management consultancy. This sounded like a good chance to exercise her analytical skills on a broad range of topics and make some decent money in the process. She was looking forward to the challenge and attacked her new job with lots of enthusiasm and hard work.

The working reality proved frustrating. In theory, the subject matter was stimulating, but in practice her job boiled down to an endless flow of administrivia. Most of her working day consisted of updating budgets, timing plans, status reports and emails. That meant non-stop typing, spreadsheets, being anchored to a computer and desperately trying to cope with an inbound volume of material that was simply too big. She might as well have been sitting in a call centre taking customer queries all day or running a rapid response email answering system. The working days got longer and longer as the months went by.

In amongst all the administration, she was rapidly losing her sense of self. A range of emotions followed. Her first reaction was to think that it was her fault that she had too much menial work to do. Perhaps others were able to plough through the same amount of tasks faster and then free up time for the more interesting stuff. But that didn't seem likely. Next up was to wonder whether this was actually what she had signed up for – perhaps this is what the job truly involved. Again, she eventually concluded, that was unlikely.

So one day she had a chat with her boss about it. 'Oh we all go through that,' said her boss. 'You can't please everybody all of the time, and you certainly can't do it all. The main thing is to do as much as you realistically can, and to do everything on your own terms. If you keep doing what everyone else wants you to do, you'll never get to do what you want to do.'

It was advice from someone who had been through it before. So she concluded that it was actually fine to decline some tasks, to manage her work as she felt fit and to get the nature of her work back to where it should be. That would mean far less administration and much more thinking about the things that really mattered. Reorienting her work in this way gave her a new lease of life and rekindled her enthusiasm for the industry she had joined.

Humility + honesty + humour = happiness

Three Hs – humility, honesty and humour – can contribute significantly to a fourth one: happiness. Being well adjusted helps you to cope with extremes, to laugh at mishaps and to shrug off adverse conditions. Humility, honesty and humour help massively in this struggle. They are your force field.

Humility, or the ability to be humble, may sound like a rather strange quality to recommend as a constituent part of technological success, but let me explain. Humility has a number of subtly different meanings – being conscious of one's failings, being unpretentious and being deferential or servile. Being conscious of one's failings is crucial. So is being unpretentious. Being servile, however, is not desirable. Why is it helpful to be conscious of one's failings in relation to technology? So that you can use it to compensate for your weaknesses. Lack of pretension is a highly desirable quality too. The world these days is full of it – full of 'better than thou' people, frequently with the condescending language to match. Talk straight and people will appreciate it hugely.

Honesty is important on four levels when it comes to taming technology.

▶ Being honest with yourself.

▶ Being honest about your approach to technology.

▶ Being honest when communicating through it.

▶ Being honest with others as an end result.

Try to analyse your technological relationship in a rational way. Try not to cloud it with inaccurate self-perception. Design an approach that suits you and that is realistic for your capability, set-up and available time. Retain your integrity when communicating with machines and regularly realign the one with the other. The net result should be that there is no difference between dealing with you direct and dealing via technology.

Humour is crucial to well-being. Read any medical bulletin and it will tell you that a good laugh is good for your health. Besides which, it makes everything more fun. Who wants to hang around with a curmudgeon? The world has its fair quota of dull, worthy people, so why would you want to join in? You don't need to wear a comedy nose all day or practise stand-up routines in front of the mirror to entertain everyone. Just view the world with a lighter touch. Awkward situations can be diffused brilliantly with a smile and a humorous attitude.

Humour and common sense go hand in hand. As William James said: 'Common sense and a sense of humour are the same thing, moving at different speeds. A sense of humour is just common sense, dancing.' Common sense is an absolutely vital ingredient in handling your technology. And as we know, it isn't all that common. A healthy sense of humour will allow you to view your interaction with machines with a wry smile. So when you have a problem with it – a technical issue, some kind of meltdown or just a misunderstanding born out of poor communication – you will be able to see it for what it is: a temporary storm that can be resolved with a laugh and the right attitude.

Duration, variation and vacation

When it comes to being, there are certain things you can do to be relentlessly enthusiastic. Keep an eye on duration, variation and vacation. That means never doing one thing for too long, having plenty of variety in what you do and going on holiday at suitable intervals. This will enable you to set your standards high, keep them there and enact them every day with a high degree of consistency.

It is a rare person who enjoys doing the same thing over and over again for a very long time. That could mean several hours at a computer on the same day. Or it could mean most days of the week for three months, or most weeks of the year for five years. The ratio doesn't matter, but the principle does. Eventually we all get bored. Consequently, it is very important that you never do one thing on a machine for too long. In the context of one working day, it is probably unhelpful for you to do one particular task for more than a couple of hours. To stay fresh, you should move on to something else unless it is one of those exceptional items that simply has to be churned through from time to time and really does take a long while. Even then, you may still need regular breaks from it and breaking up any monotonous task is a healthy thing to do.

In any particular working week, you really do not want to be having the same technological encounter every day. You can keep it up for a while, but not for months. Keep reminding yourself that you are the person in charge. If your work is becoming repetitive, change it. Benjamin Franklin decreed that 'The definition of insanity is doing the same thing over and over again and expecting different results.' If that's you, then you need to engineer a set-up that keeps you sane. To recap:

▶ Keep lots of variety in what you do to stay fresh.

▶ Change things if you don't find them interesting.

▶ Take regular breaks and a sensible amount of time off.

Remember this

We can all be better by defining our own characters and not allowing them to be defined by technology.

If you do this you will be able to approach all your dealings with technology energetically and enthusiastically. That's the vital importance of balance in your life. So to recap, you need to look carefully at the five areas and make some technological resolutions:

Thinking. *We don't do enough of it, even though it's completely free. Events overtake us. We need to rediscover the art of thinking clearly and use it to improve our quality of life.*

Talking. *We do too much of it, often without having thought first. We talk too much rubbish and not enough sense. It's time* *for a new, more considered approach that reflects what we feel more accurately and makes it easier for others to understand us.*

Communicating. *We have so many methods of communicating available to us that we frequently choose the wrong one. We need the right medium for the right message and a clear understanding of the suitability of each for the task.*

Doing. *We do far too much of the wrong stuff, which often means we do not have enough time left for the right stuff. We need to be able to distinguish between what matters and what doesn't to make better use of our time.*

Being. *We can all be better. We should define our own characters, not allow them to be defined by our possessions or technology. Having a better life starts with knowing what you are all about and emanating that style.*

It's time to tame technology and get your life back. As Bob Dylan said: 'A man is a success if he gets up in the morning and gets to bed at night, and in between he does what he wants to.'

Taming Technology Tips for Being

1 **Define your character and style**

   Take the time to define and understand what you are all about. Only then will you be able to plan and enact your relationship with your technology. Try assessing this with no reference at all to technology. This may be harder than you expect.

2 **Consider the idea of eudaemonia**

   It's a big word but it's not a complicated idea. Work out how the way you behave with your machines affects your happiness and make changes based on what you conclude. Aim for a rational, active life, with the emphasis on the rational when it comes to technology. Design this is as you would like it to be, not as it currently is, most likely pressurized by too many devices and too much demand on your time.

3 **As far as possible, only do technological things that you like**

   Your work may force you to do some things that you don't particularly enjoy, but try to keep this to a minimum and certainly do not replicate these tasks in your free time. Using technology for recreation is fine, so long as it doesn't drive your family to distraction. Consider what you truly enjoy doing and try to strike an acceptable balance.

4 When it comes to machines, do not distinguish between nice and nasty things to do

Many people try to predict whether a task will be nice or nasty. Often they are proven wrong, so it wasn't worth worrying about anyway. Some things just have to be done and there's no getting away from it. Review how technology can do these tasks for you and so relieve the burden. If it can't, then just get on with it. And don't put things off – they usually get worse if you do.

5 Remind yourself of all the positive things that technology can do

Imagine a world in which none of your technology existed. Have a think about how difficult certain tasks would be without it. Use that as a reminder of how helpful a lot of it is. Then concentrate on the difference between those areas where technology really helps and those where it can actually cause problems. Pledge to emphasize the helpful examples and remove as many of the unhelpful ones as far as possible.

6 Never use a piece of technology unless you know why you are using it

More thought and less diving in. Many of us have irrational habits and the way we use our technology may well be one of them. Don't take this for granted. If you find yourself using a piece of technology and then suddenly wondering why, stop immediately. Pause, reflect and consider if there is another way to tackle the issue.

7 Use humility, honesty and humour to create happiness

The four Hs are a powerful blend. Recognize your failings and use technology to compensate for them. Be honest with yourself and your relationship with your devices. Have a laugh more often. You'll be happier.

8 Keep a careful eye on duration, variation and vacation

Don't do anything for too long, keep things varied and take breaks at suitable intervals. You can't spend your life nailed to a machine. There have been genuine examples of people who have died from sitting at a computer too long. Set an alarm if you need to – take a breather and do something else for a while.

9 **Smaller chunks of technology mean greater clarity**
   Don't be seduced by huge projects. Pose a problem, solve it with the most relevant machine and then move on to the next (preferably small) thing. Tearing at a large task with just one approach doesn't always work. Use the right tool for each element of the job.

10 **Take the issues seriously, but not yourself**
   No further explanation should be needed. Things can be serious, but you don't have to be. It will be alright, honestly.

Focus points

✻ Are you defined by your character or your technology? Too much time spent attached to machines can be bad for the soul. Take the time to pause and reflect on what you are doing. Taming your technology may be necessary.

✻ Getting your attitude right is important. Many people these days are slaves to their machines. If this is at work, consider carefully how you can vary your tasks or make the nature of them more tolerable. More employers are becoming acutely aware of this problem, so you probably won't be alone.

✻ Humility + honesty + humour = happiness. It's an equation with important components. Too many people use technology to boast, fudge the truth, or become overly serious or aggressive. Subsuming these tendencies will most likely increase your chances of being happy and calm.

✻ Keep a careful eye on the duration of your technological interactions. Even if it's essential that you are working with machines, you need to take regular breaks. That also goes for changing the nature of your tasks (variation) and making sure that you don't become so engrossed in projects that you fail to take appropriate time off – whether that's going home on time, not working the weekend or making sure you take your vacation.

✻ Try some of the Taming Technology Tips for Being. Start with one or two. If they work, keep going. If they don't, try some others.

Epilogue: Two Visions of the Future

A dystopian vision of the future: technology rules – and it's bad

It's 2025 and everything George Orwell predicted in his book *1984* has come to pass – with a twist. There's no nasty Big Brother in charge as such, but technology has completely taken over and the will of man has been suppressed beneath the yolk of the machine. Man invented the machine, but now the invented has usurped the inventor. It affects all aspects of life, from the home to the office. What's happening?

The original big dream for technology only happened in part. The bit that did happen was the invention of a range of machines that could do extraordinary things – things that could remove the drudgery from humans and free them up to do more interesting stuff. In the 1970s and 1980s, the prediction was that our standard working life of 100,000 hours would reduce as a result to 50,000 hours. By the 2000s, the machines had indeed come to pass, but the result wasn't what the humans intended. The ability to get more done went up, but the working hours didn't decrease, they stayed the same – in fact, in some countries, such as the USA, they actually went up.

The benefits of the technology were sold and promoted hard to an eager populace, who lapped it all up and paid a lot of money for it – both corporate and personal. Mobile phones started as a convenience for emergencies, morphed into lifestyle accessories and eventually ended up as multi-media devices that led to ediction and an 'always on' mentality. Executives complained that they were never entirely free from the grasp of their employers and yet they refused to turn their handsets off.

Bastardized language led to the decline of proper communication. Text messages reduced language to a sht fm of wds tht lst mng ovr th yrs. Relationships floundered as a result. CCTV recorded every move, particularly in the UK, which generated a higher concentration of cameras than any other country in the world. One person's word against another became a thing of the past – it was all recorded. The cloud was shown to be the charade that a few suspected it was – merely a cleaner sounding way of describing hundreds of square miles of heavily polluting server farms generating inordinate amounts of heat and contributing to global warming.

Email culture effectively killed communication in the workplace and replaced it with a 'pass the buck' mechanism on an unprecedented scale. Oppressed executives merely had to point to an order to a subordinate on a screen to prove that it wasn't their fault. People were fired as a result. The machines knew everything. Technology became the default place from which to receive orders. Instructions from bosses were no longer delivered in person – merely issued by machine. An employee would pick up his or her tasks for the day and enact them, delivering the output electronically.

Technology ruled, and for humans, it was bad.

In all of this, humans lost their soul. Dictated to by, or at the very least via, machines, they lost their mental centre of gravity. As the sociable element of company life ebbed to a trickle, the spark of creativity dried up to be replaced by a set of formulaic instructions. Functional replaced fantastical. Creativity was no longer required, so long as the job got done.

A utopian vision of the future: technology is everywhere – and it's good

It's 2025. Humans have invented some extraordinary types of technology and the good news is that the balance between who does what and who gets told what to do is a good one. Some cynics suggested that everything would work out like George

Orwell's *1984*, with the people being subsumed under some tyrannical system enabled by ever-watchful machines. But it didn't work out like that.

Sure, there were machines that could, if instructed, monitor your every move, but the good guys won and the machines were only used to keep criminals at bay. Ubiquitous security cameras, DNA databases and security coding meant that crime was well down all over the world. Robots were now universally available and could perform all the boring menial tasks that most humans don't like – household chores, sorting out the post, walking the dog, paying the bills and so on. Want the garden watered? Fine – just programme the homebot to do the honours.

Systems that never used to work now did. The railways now ran on time and with supreme efficiency thanks to driverless trains run on a digitally controlled network. Home deliveries happened on time because they ran on a monorail to depots with the final mile being fulfilled by robots armed with barcodes. Not in to receive a delivery? No problem – it will be left in the secure storage bin outside your house, accessible only by your unique PIN code.

At last humans get the chance to do the sorts of things they have always wanted to. For office workers, going home on time is now not only possible, but compulsory. Email quantities are now limited to the daily ISA maximum – the International Standard Amount that all businesses agreed was the most an individual could realistically cope with in one day. Anyone trying to send someone more than that would receive a bounceback saying 'Wait till tomorrow for this task' or 'This person is overloaded today – please reconsider your request'.

Hobbies and health were on the up as individuals finally had time for recreational sports and hobbies. Regardless of climate, most world cities now had ski slopes, rivers and lakes for water sports, and artificially created rock structures for climbing. Divorce rates were down as couples had more time to spend with each other and communicate properly. Crime was down because people were essentially happier.

Doubters were worried that having machines replacing so many menial tasks would oust the 'common man' from lower status jobs, but it never happened. Dreary, functional tasks were indeed performed by robots and the average person was delighted to be relieved of the drudgery. These people were instead able to create a new level of worker – a mixture of blue- and white-collar worker that some dubbed 'baby blue'. They were freed from monotonous administrivia and liberated to use their brains. Societies found that allowing so-called 'unqualified' people to solve problems actually increased GDP across the world.

Looming world issues could be better solved collectively rather than by an elite bunch of scientists or a government think tank. When grappling with poverty, unemployment, food shortages, climate change, social inequality, disease, and almost every other charity-based subject, the new approach showed that freeing up people to solve problems rather than bogging them down in manual labour reaped great dividends and was more than viable.

Technology was everywhere, and for humans, it was good.

References

CHAPTER 1

Affluenza, Oliver James (Random House, 2007)

Cognitive Surplus, Clay Shirky (Allen Lane, 2010)

Enough, John Naish (Hodder & Stoughton, 2008)

Faster, James Gleick (Abacus, 1999)

National Phobics Society Survey (2009)

Socialnomics, Erik Qualman (John Wiley, 2009)

The Age Of Unreason, Charles Handy (Arrow, 1989)

The Paradox of Choice, Barry Schwartz (Harper Perennial, 2004)

The Play Ethic, Pat Kane (Pan, 2004)

The Selfish Capitalist, Oliver James (Vermillion, 2008)

CHAPTER 2

American Journal of Psychiatry (2010)

Cyburbia, James Harkin (Little Brown, 2009)

Generation Me (Association for Psychological Science, 2010)

HotJobs Yahoo Survey (May 2009)

Information Anxiety, Richard Saul Wurman (Bantam, 1990)

In Search of the Obvious, Jack Trout (John Wiley, 2008)

Internet Innovation Alliance (2010)

Sunday Times (29 March 2009)

The Cost Of Multitasking, Ophir & Nass (Stanford University, 2010)

The Little Big Things, Tom Peters (Harper Collins, 2010)

The Shallows: What the internet is doing to our brains, Nicholas Carr (Blackstone, 2010)

The Times (31 June 2009, 8 May 2010)

The Tyranny of Email, John Freeman (Simon Spotlight, 2009)

CHAPTER 3

Execution, Bossidy & Sharan (Crown Business, 2002)

Introducing Psychology, Nigel Benson (Icon, 1998)

Small Business Survival, Kevin Duncan (Hodder & Stoughton, 2010)

So What?, Kevin Duncan (Capstone, 2008)

The Cost Of Multitasking, Ophir & Nass (Stanford University, 2010)

The God Delusion, Richard Dawkins (Black Swan, 2007)

The Tipping Point, Malcolm Gladwell (Little Brown, 2000)

CHAPTER 4

High Impact Speeches, Richard Heller (Pearson, 2003)

Rework, Fried & Hansson (Vermillion, 2010)

Tick Achieve (Capstone, 2008)

CHAPTER 5

Business Greatest Hits, Kevin Duncan (A&C Black, 2010)

Getting Things Done, David Allen (Piatkus, 2001)

Run Your Own Business, Kevin Duncan (Hodder & Stoughton, 2010)

The Paradox of Choice, Barry Schwartz (Harper Perennial, 2004)

The Tyranny of Email, John Freeman (Simon Spotlight, 2009)

CHAPTER 6

Do Nothing, New York Times (9 March 2010)

How To Be Idle, Tom Hodgkinson (Penguin, 2004)

How To Get More Done, Fergus O'Connell (Pearson, 2008)

Marketing Greatest Hits, Kevin Duncan (A&C Black, 2010)

Sticky Wisdom, Matt Kingdon et al. (Capstone, 2002)

The Seven-Day Weekend, Ricardo Semler (Century, 2003)

Whatever You Think, Think The Opposite, Paul Arden (Penguin, 2006)

CHAPTER 7

Obliquity, John Kay (Profile, 2010)

Small Business Survival, Kevin Duncan (Hodder & Stoughton, 2010)

Start, Kevin Duncan (Capstone, 2008)

Index

We hope you have enjoyed this book. The following chapter is a sample from the same author's previous book:

Start Your Own Business In A Week

SUNDAY

Getting
started

It's a daunting prospect, isn't it? An empty desk, no customers, no confirmed money coming in, and no one to gossip with. Welcome to running your own business! Every issue is now yours to wrestle with, and yours alone. But then so is all the satisfaction – mental and financial – when things are going well. Today we are going to work out exactly how you are going to turn what many would regard as an ordeal into the start of a fantastic success.

We are going to look at:

- how to be honest with yourself about your offer
- what you need to prepare in order to be a success
- how to write a simple, realistic plan
- working out the materials that you need
- how to get it all under way.

Assume that you have something to offer

'The beginning is half of every action.'
Greek proverb

Let's start by assuming that there is a market for your talents; otherwise you wouldn't have got this far. We have to believe that this is true because you probably wouldn't be reading this book unless you were convinced that you have something to offer. By now you will have established the basics in your mind. Your thought pattern will have been something along the lines of:

- I am good at what I do.
- I believe that there is a market for my product or service. (Whether this is actually true, and how you set about proving it to yourself, will come a little later.)
- I can do my job better on my own than in my current set-up.
- I have a way of doing my job that people will like.
- What I put in alongside what I get out will be a better-balanced equation than my current state of affairs.

Thousands of people go through this thought process at some point in their working lives – sometimes on many occasions. However, even if you have been able to tick all the boxes so far, the issue that you have to grapple with next is far more fundamental: 'If I ran my own business, I'm not sure if I could live with myself.'

When people say this, they mean that they are thinking about important issues such as where exactly they are going to do their work and what their domestic arrangements are. Could they possibly accommodate getting everything done that they need to without disrupting all the other aspects of their life?

Secondly, there is your frame of mind: are you cut out to operate outside a conventional office environment? Could you cope without the interaction? Could you motivate yourself when

SUNDAY
MONDAY
TUESDAY
WEDNESDAY
THURSDAY
FRIDAY
SATURDAY

no one is giving you a kick up the backside? It is essential that you feel good about yourself and what you have to offer.

Feel good about your offer
You must genuinely believe that you can offer something of value to others; otherwise you should not take the plunge to start up on your own, or even be toying with the idea.

Be honest with yourself

Do remember, however, that confidence can be misplaced. In fact, over-confidence could beguile you into believing that you have a viable idea or a successful way of doing things when in fact you don't, so confront your own hubris and work it out privately before it trips you up.

You are starting your own business now, so you shouldn't have to pretend about anything. In fact, you mustn't ever stray into the realms of fantasy, because you would only be fooling yourself if you did. From now on it is your job to be sensible and realistic. Don't exaggerate your potential or delude yourself that you can do all sorts of things that you cannot. Equally, do not be sheepish about your skills. You will need to get used to showing a fascinating blend of confidence and humility.

Consider your position with extreme care and as much objectivity as you can muster. Get a piece of paper. Write down what you want to do in your business. Stare at it for a bit, and then decide whether anyone else would agree with you. This is the beginning of establishing whether there is indeed a market for what you do. Go for a walk. When you come back, stare at your piece of paper again. Is your idea any good? Is it nonsense? If so, write a new one. Stick it on the wall and live with it for a few days. Does it still make sense? Is it rubbish? Does everyone else claim the same thing? What's so different about the way that you would run your business? These early enquiries are really important.

Research your market thoroughly

If you reckon you have an excellent idea, the first essential thing to do is to research your market thoroughly. Actually it isn't one thing to do – it's a lot of things. Try asking yourself these sorts of questions:

- What demand is there for what I provide?
  - If I am producing a product, who wants to buy it?
  - If I am providing a service, who needs it?
- Who else in the area does this already? (This could be geographical or sector-based.)
  - Are they a success? If so, why?
  - Are they a failure? If so, what does that tell me?
- What price can I put on my product or service?
  - Does that represent a going concern or will I be hard-pushed to make a living?
- What outside factors am I subject to?
  - Can I influence these factors, or am I totally at their mercy?
  - If I have no control over them, does that make the whole venture too vulnerable?
- If I were someone else, would I embark on this venture?
  - If so, why?

The questions are endless, but try to be like an inquisitive child and always ask *why?* three times in relation to every question.

Work out how much money you need

What is required here is not a forest of spreadsheets but just a really clear impression of how your business will work financially. Put simply, there are three types of money that you will need:

1 Initial investment
2 Monthly cash flow
3 The profit margin

Initial investment

Do you need to put any money in at all at the beginning? Just pause on this one for a moment. If the answer is no, then don't do it.

If you do need to borrow from some other source, what demands will they make on getting it back? Banks want interest. Investors want cash back. They don't do it out of kindness.

If you really do conclude that you have to put money in yourself, when are you going to get it back? Don't delude yourself by excluding this amount from your assessment of whether the business is going to be a success.

Monthly cash flow

Next comes the monthly cash flow or the amount of income you need each month. Write down what you need. Now write down what you think you can get. Then build in time delays for late payment in the early days. This becomes your first cash flow projection. This has to be very, very realistic. You have to have a reasonable level of confidence that it is achievable otherwise you will have a disaster on your hands almost straight away. You need to distinguish carefully between income and profit. Income is not profit. You can have an infinite amount of income and yet still be making a whopping loss.

Calculate how much you need to make each month. Once you write it down, it's more likely to happen. You can have a sensible minimum and maximum, but it's better if you have just one figure. Now you have to work out where it's coming from. Write down a realistic list of the value of your income in the first three months. If this turns out to be nonsense, write a more realistic list next time. As you become better at predicting this, you will naturally build in time lags to reflect slow decision-making and slow payment.

The profit margin

The third thing is the profit margin. Ask yourself:

- How much is it?
- Does it vary depending on what I've sold?
- Does it vary by month or season?
- Does it fluctuate wildly and, if so, why?
- What would make it more consistent?
- What would make it higher?
- What are the tolerance levels?
- What is the average target?
- Is that realistic?
- Is it good enough for me?

You need to keep a regular and close eye on this. You also need to have decided whether you need the margin monthly, annually, or over any other time period.

If you need it monthly, does this mean that your business plan does not include an amount for your own salary? If so, consider whether that is wise or realistic.

If you can take the profit annually, how are you keeping tabs on the surplus that you hope is building up? Can you equate it back to the running monthly amount?

The overall rule is to keep all this very simple.

Write a simple, realistic plan

Quite a few people starting a business write endless business plans before they start, and there's nothing fundamentally wrong with that. However, it's easy to get so involved in the spreadsheets and the financial projections of a plan that you lose sight of the basics. The best business plans can often be written on the back of an envelope, usually in your local café or bar. Try this simple process:

1 Write JFMAMJJASOND along the top of the page to represent the 12 months of the year.
2 Now cross out at least one or two of them because you will be taking some holiday and in the first year the whole thing will probably grind to a halt when you are not around.
3 Now write a figure under each month to determine your income.
4 Put the likely costs under each.
5 Subtract one from the other and see what you have left.
6 If you want to be particularly cautious, try crossing out the first three months' income because businesses always take longer to get off the ground than you think.
7 Now go and do something else for a while.
8 Come back to your plan and ask yourself again: 'Is this realistic?'

This exercise will tell you something a great deal more fundamental than a meeting with the bank or your accountant. It will be a big surprise if you are happy with it first time. In fact, if you are, you should be a bit suspicious. Live with it for a while. Try again. Make refinements (not on a spreadsheet, just in pen on another envelope). The great joy with this is that, by keeping it simple, you are now able to explain your business plan to anyone who will listen – and that includes you. Now, assuming that you have concluded that you do indeed have a going concern, there are some things that you will need to get under way.

Invest in a distinctive identity

You need to look good. Your company, shop or service needs a memorable name, a good logo, high-quality headed paper, good-quality signage and business cards that invoke a reaction. The name may well be your own if you are known in your field. If not, choose something distinctive. Avoid bland sets of initials that no one can remember (such as BLTWP) or hugely cumbersome stacks of names like Jones, Duncan, Taylor, Hatstand European Consolidated & Partners. They are not memorable and they imply a lack of clarity on your part.

Every detail counts. Don't skimp on quality of paper or thickness of business cards. Thin business cards are as weak as a limp handshake. Don't have them done at a booth in a railway station! Check the spelling and punctuation really carefully on everything you produce. These days, the world appears to be one large typographical error. Don't be part of it.

When you are describing your business, don't tell people that you haven't really made your mind up about what you want to do, or that you are 'just giving it a go to see what happens'. If you are indecisive about your own concern, you may well unwittingly give the impression that you will be indecisive or unreliable when dealing with your customers. And why would anyone want to do business with someone who has already let you know that they might not be around for long? Customers are much more likely to be loyal to businesses that are reliable and consistent in their own right.

Get connected

These days, computers are an essential element of almost every business. They are not there to ruin your life but to make it easier. Put all your information in your personal organizer and computer, and back them up regularly on disk to avoid calamity. (Put these back-up reminders in your diary now.) Think carefully about what you want your computer to do for your business, and choose your system accordingly.

● What information might you want to retrieve at some point in the future?
● What might your customers want to know?
● What might you want to know?
● What about your accountant or the dreaded taxman?
● What is the best way of cataloguing your records?
● What is the simplest way of doing all this?

TIP Make technology work for you
Don't design your system around what the technology can do. Instead, decide what you want from it and design something around those needs. Some careful thought at this stage could save you hours of heartache in the future.

Appoint a good accountant

There are whole books on this one subject, but let's just stick to the basics. You really do need to know how to arrange all your financial affairs from the beginning. You won't want to discover at the end of the year that you have been recording information in the wrong way and that you now have to reorganize everything.

Decide what you need, and organize all your money matters in the easiest possible way. Meeting your accountant once a year should be sufficient, with a few telephone calls every now and then to clarify any details. Keep it simple and think ahead. If you have money problems looming, address them early. Never succumb to the terrible practice of shoving bills in a problem drawer and ignoring them for months – you will create mounting debt and establish a reputation for not paying your suppliers. This is the slippery slope to bankruptcy.

Depending on the nature of your business, here are some of the gritty financial issues that must be addressed right at the beginning.

- Will you be a sole trader or will you register as a company at Companies House?
- Do you need separate bank accounts and, if so, how many?
- How will your tax affairs be arranged?
- Which elements of the business need to be kept financially separate?
- Do you need to rearrange parts of your current personal money habits to adjust to the new set-up?
- Do you need to register for VAT?
- Have you considered national insurance?
- What is the optimum system for paying the lowest amount of tax?

SUNDAY

MONDAY

TUESDAY

WEDNESDAY

THURSDAY

FRIDAY

SATURDAY

Work out the materials you need

You need to work out precisely what materials you need to run your business. This sounds rather basic but a surprising number of people start their business without really addressing this issue. For example, if you are running a retail outlet, you need to resolve such questions as:

● What stock do I need?
● How much investment is that?
● How quickly can I reorder?
● Do I know where from?
● Do I have the contacts?
● Where will stock be stored?
● Is it safe and secure?
● Is it insured?
● What system will I have for knowing when I am running out?
● Are there legal requirements that I need to take into account?

If you are selling a service, you will need to have as a minimum a clear description of what you are offering cogently written down. This might be in the form of a brochure containing your CV, a client list, some examples of your skills and a list of things that could be of interest to a potential customer.

You will certainly need to state your terms of business. Most businesses start without these and only draw some up after their first debt. But the smart person has them from the beginning to set a precedent and head off financial problems from the off.

Here is a basic checklist of the tools you will need:

● Description of your business   ❑
● Your CV   ❑
● Your clients   ❑
● Examples of what you offer   ❑
● Examples of what you have done for others   ❑
● Prices   ❑
● Terms of business   ❑

Network constantly

The main burden of letting people know that you are open for business falls on you. You therefore need to overcome any shyness or reservations you may have about marketing your business.

Have business cards on you all the time, even for social occasions. This is where you may pick up much of your work. Once you start chatting, you'll find that most people are interested in what you do. Without forcing your product or service on them, you will be able always to seem professional by letting them know what you offer and having your contact details to hand.

There's a huge difference between basic marketing and being irritating. Calm, professional marketers state what they do in a clear, charming way. If the reaction of the other person is reasonably positive, they might hand over a card. It's amazing how, months later, the phone rings and a potential new customer says, 'I met you once and now I have a need for what you do...'

> *'Far and away the best prize that life offers is the chance to work hard at work worth doing.'*
>
> Theodore Roosevelt

Summary

Today has been about assuming that you have something to offer, banishing doubts, and working out why anyone should buy what you provide or produce. Being honest with yourself is crucial, because self-deception at this stage will lead to trouble later.

Researching your market thoroughly is important, because someone else may have already used that great idea you had in the pub. Work out how much money you need, and write a simple, realistic plan. Many a launch has been paralysed by constantly reworking the figures, so make clear decisions and move reasonably fast. Invest in a distinctive identity and make sure yours doesn't look the same as anybody else's.

Get connected, because you can't work in a vacuum. Appoint a good accountant – if you mess up the accounts at the beginning, it will cost a lot more to unravel them later. Work out the materials you need, and network constantly without being irritating – people can't use you if they don't know you're there.

Now you must make it happen: inertia ruins many a business.

SUNDAY
MONDAY
TUESDAY
WEDNESDAY
THURSDAY
FRIDAY
SATURDAY

Fact-check [answers at the back]

1. When starting your own business, what's the right attitude to have?
   a) A conviction that I have something to offer ❏
   b) Someone else will do all the work ❏
   c) It'll never work ❏
   d) I'm not much good at what I do ❏

2. How do you set about researching your market?
   a) A quick skim should do the trick ❏
   b) Ask around, but don't worry about checking too much detail ❏
   c) Do it thoroughly, using every source possible ❏
   d) Do none and leave it to chance ❏

3. When it comes to money, what should you do?
   a) Some rough calculations and then get started ❏
   b) Spend months generating lots of spreadsheets ❏
   c) Work out precisely how much money you need ❏
   d) Calculate the first bit and then do the rest later ❏

4. What's the best way to write a business plan?
   a) Write a long, complicated one ❏
   b) Get someone else to do it ❏
   c) Copy someone else's ❏
   d) Write a simple, realistic one ❏

5. When it comes to your company identity, what should you do?
   a) Avoid the cost altogether ❏
   b) Imitate someone else's ❏
   c) Invest in a distinctive one ❏
   d) Go for a cheap one ❏

6. When deciding how connected to make your business, what should you do?
   a) Get thoroughly connected ❏
   b) Go for the bare minimum ❏
   c) Assume business will come to you ❏
   d) Just use traditional methods ❏

7. What's the right approach to accountants?
   a) Avoid them – they're too expensive ❏
   b) Use one occasionally ❏
   c) Appoint a good one ❏
   d) Appoint one without much research ❏

8. What's the best approach to materials?
   a) Work it out as you go along ❏
   b) Work out everything you need at the beginning ❏
   c) Just get the bare minimum to start with ❏
   d) Ignore it – something will crop up ❏

9. What should your approach to networking be?
a) Network constantly without being irritating ☐
b) Don't bother – it's not worth it ☐
c) Network with anyone you can get hold of ☐
d) Just do it occasionally ☐

10. What's the right approach to making things happen?
a) Delegate to someone else ☐
b) It'll happen eventually ☐
c) Put it off and hope it all works out ☐
d) It's my business so it's my job to get it done ☐

SUNDAY
MONDAY
TUESDAY
WEDNESDAY
THURSDAY
FRIDAY
SATURDAY